# A Survival Guide *for* Working *with* Humans

*Dealing with Whiners, Back-Stabbers, Know-It-Alls, and Other Difficult People*

## GINI GRAHAM SCOTT, PH.D.

AMERICAN MANAGEMENT ASSOCIATION
New York | Atlanta | Brussels | Chicago | Mexico City | San Francisco
Shanghai | Tokyo | Toronto | Washington D.C.

Special discounts on bulk quantities of AMACOM books are available to corporations, professional associations, and other organizations. For details, contact Special Sales Department, AMACOM, a division of American Management Association, 1601 Broadway, New York, NY 10019.
Tel.: 212-903-8316. Fax: 212-903-8083.
Web site: www.amacombooks.org

This publication is designed to provide accurate and authoritative information in regard to the subject matter covered. It is sold with the understanding that the publisher is not engaged in rendering legal, accounting, or other professional service. If legal advice or other expert assistance is required, the services of a competent professional person should be sought.

Library of Congress Cataloging-in-Publication Data

Scott, Gini Graham.
A survival guide for working with humans : dealing with whiners.
back-stabbers, know-it-alls, and other difficult people / Gini Graham
Scott.
    p. cm.
Includes bibliographical references and index.
ISBN-10: 0-8144-7205-2
ISBN-13: 978-0-8144-7205-7
1. Conflict management.   2. Interpersonal relations.   3. Interpersonal
conflict.   I. Title.
HD42.S358   2004
650.1'3   dc22                                              2003020908

Printing number

10   9   8   7   6

# Contents

# Acknowledgments

I want to extend my thanks to the many people who contributed to this book, especially to:

My editor at AMACOM, Jacquie Flynn, who helped guide the process of turning what began as newspaper columns in a dozen papers into a book. She offered many insights and was always cheerful and fun to work with.

My copyeditor, Barbara Chernow, who made the review process a breeze.

The agent I worked with on this book, Mike Valentino, at Cambridge Literary, who handled the follow-up and contract details, after I sent out an initial query through publishersandagents.net.

And to the many people, who must remain unnamed, who described their own workplace problems and conflicts and asked for advice.

Gini Graham Scott

# Introduction

Today, with a sputtering economy, collapsing and merging companies, corporate scandals, high-tech upheavals, and growing global competition, life in the workplace is more difficult than ever. Trusting in business relationships has become more uncertain, too.

It helps to have guidelines on how to maneuver through today's unpredictable work environment, much like learning to swim through a narrow chasm in a swirling river.

That's what *A Survival Guide for Working with Humans* is all about. It started with a series of mostly weekly columns in the San Francisco Bay Area on the perils of the workplace and what to do about them. Eventually my editor had to drop the columns to run more advertising and specialty features, but as reader response grew I decided to expand on the idea for these columns and turn them into a book. In a sense, I decided to take my own advice: to find a way to turn a problem into an opportunity and look for ways to put a positive spin on whatever happens. Indeed the columns themselves were inspired after a long-term relationship with a difficult client went south, and my solution to the problem ended up as the topic of one of the first columns.

Then, as I heard from readers, I saw how my own approach helped others. It's based on using a method I developed through consulting, doing workshops and seminars, and writing books on a wide range of topics—from becoming more creative to making choices, solving problems, dealing with change, and resolving conflicts and ethical dilemmas. This approach reflects a mix of using problem solving and conflict resolution techniques, along with employing methods such as visualization, mental gymnastics, and intuitive reasoning to decide the best approach. It also features an emphasis on using common sense and playing fair—but at the same time accepts the need to be aggressive and even devious when confronting a stacked deck. Other basic principles include seeking clear communications, promoting increased productivity along with improved morale and relationships, and contributing to the common good while helping yourself. In short, this approach is a combination pragmatic/ethical, intuitive/rational, follow-the-rules but know-when-to-make-or-break-them method that makes work and business, as well as personal relationships, more successful.

What's important in using these methods is to recognize that no one size fits all, and different principles, strategies, and tactics will work best for you at different times. But as you think about how other people have applied these techniques and principles, you'll start thinking how you might use them yourself in different situations, with different people, and for different purposes.

So consider these chapters as a series of recipes for coming up with a better way of dealing with your everyday experiences at work and in business relationships. It's the first in a series of books of recipes for success, which cover questions on everything from how to remake yourself in a more diversified workplace to how to deal with backstabbing, gossip, poor communication, and even when to bring in the lawyers or go to court.

In keeping with this recipe approach, each chapter includes:

 An introductory paragraph highlighting the problem.

 A short story or a couple of stories about one or more people who faced this problem (with their identities and companies concealed, of course).

A quiz with a list of possible responses so you can think about what you might do; you can even use this as a game to discuss this issue with others and compare your responses.

 A discussion about what people did to resolve their problems successfully or what they might do.

 A series of three or more take-aways to highlight what to learn from the chapter.

I hope you find that the short, snappy, conversational style of this survival guide makes it fun and quick to read, even if some of the problems are ones you haven't encountered.

So now, dig in. Feel free to explore and try out these different recipes in any order as you learn and think about how to increase your workplace survivor-ability quotient—your SAQ for short. Plus, if you have your own questions—feel free to visit my Web site and ask for answers to your own questions—at *www.workingwithhumans.com*.

# PART I

## *An*
# Aggressive
# Species

# 1
# When Sweet Revenge Isn't So Sweet

Sometimes the notion of "sweet revenge" can seem so fitting. Someone has promised to meet your deadline at work but hasn't come through despite repeated assurances. A boss has unreasonably threatened penalties if you don't meet a deadline for completing a lengthy report for his presentation with new clients, and then doesn't give you credit when you do come through. A client tells you she's going to hire you to work on her next project after you put in long hours to do a really great job, but later she instead hires a friend.

You may be thinking that sweet revenge might be just the ticket to get back at those who wrong you, particularly if you believe no one will know what you did, say if you send an anonymous letter or phone in an anonymous tip to a regulatory agency or company higher-up. Or perhaps you believe you might benefit yourself while undermining your adversary by acting like a genuinely concerned person providing others with a helpful, altruistic warning about the person who did you wrong, to keep them from getting hurt..

But think again. Sometimes sweet revenge isn't so sweet, and the fire you start can come back and burn you severely.

That's what happened to Betty when she contacted Jane, a recently hired outside PR person, to get product information for a company newsletter she was writing. The newsletter featured the latest news about what different departments in the company were doing and information on useful services that anyone in the company might find helpful. The PR person was representing a gourmet foods company as well as Betty's own company. Betty had just written an overview about companies that offered these gourmet delivery services, and now she wanted a sample of a typical lunch delivery, such as a few mouth-watering gourmet sandwiches and deserts, to include a personal reaction in her article. In fact, her boss asked her to add this personal touch.

But then Betty ran into problems with Jane, the PR person for the service, when she asked Jane for a product sample. After some back and forth e-mails and phone calls, Jane said she would check with the service about messengering the sample over in time to make Betty's deadline. But a few hours later, just before Betty's deadline, Jane sent another e-mail telling Betty she couldn't do anything to help and Betty should find someone in the company who actually made the food packages, since the gourmet food service only delivered them. Then, she concluded her memo on a note of exasperation, saying that this was really an inappropriate unprofessional request, and Betty's company should simply purchase the service if it wanted product samples. Her response infuriated Betty, since Jane had left her hanging for hours before saying she couldn't do something and on top of that impugned Betty's integrity. Though the amount involved was small, PR companies commonly provided samples when they were going to gain a plug for the product or service of the company they represented, and usually PR representatives were only too happy to act as liaisons between the person writing the article and the company providing the product or service. Betty was livid that not only was Jane not acting as people usually did in this situation, but she was also making Betty seem at fault, even unethical, for making what was an ordinary request. Now, because of Jane's delay in getting back to her, Betty might not make her deadline to get the information for the article.

Betty exploded, feeling not only stonewalled but also insulted. Why couldn't Jane have referred her to the appropriate contact in the first place, or, better yet, given her the number? And why did Jane accuse her of being rude and unprofessional, when she felt Jane's note and behavior was far more offensive than anything she might have done? After Betty called the food company's contact and got the delivery in time to make her deadline, she stewed about how to handle what Jane had done. She felt driven to do something to release her pent up rage, and she began asking her friends, family, and associates for advice, or, more accurately, for support for her desire to take action to get back at Jane.

Betty mulled over the possibilities, in her own mind and with others. She considered writing a nasty letter to Jane telling her off for her own "rude and unprofessional" e-mail and unhelpful behavior. Or even better, Betty liked the idea of calling Jane's boss at her small PR firm representing the food service company to complain that Jane was insulting to her and initially unhelpful in connecting her to the other company that provided the food. Betty even justified the exposé she planned to her friends, explaining that this revelation might help Jane's boss know that Jane was unhelpful, and her behavior might interfere with the company getting favorable exposure for their clients in future articles. In her mind, Betty thought she would appear altruistic, even as she savored how Jane might lose her job.

Yet should Betty do anything at all to get back at Jane? Should she really act to gain some sweet revenge? Unfortunately, for all the fleeting satisfaction she might feel at whatever she did, the downside is that any effort at revenge could easily backfire. For instance, an angry e-mail or phone call could lead to an escalating war of words, while contacting Jane's employer could come off as mean and vindictive, particularly since Jane was a new PR person, just learning the ropes.

So what should Betty do?

## What Should Betty Do?

Here are some possibilities. In Betty's place, what would you do and why? What do you think the outcomes of these different options would be?

 Send a frank letter to Jane, telling her how her own behavior was rude and unprofessional, so Jane will understand what she did wrong and shape up in the future.

Call Jane's boss to let him know about Jane's failings, so he can tell Jane to shape up or ship out.

 Call up Jane and arrange to have a heart-to-heart talk to explain how you felt she was unhelpful and rude, hoping she'll understand, apologize, and improve her act in the future.

 Send an anonymous letter to Jane's boss to advise him to watch Jane more closely, since she was not doing her job very well, without giving specific details.

 Send a friendly e-mail thanking Jane for the referral to the other company, and then diplomatically point out that you were working to meet a deadline for your boss and that your company has gotten such samples from other companies before, so there was nothing untoward about your remark. Then, invite Jane to call you if she wants to discuss this further, since your company may be working with her PR company in the future, so the two of you may have to work together again.

 Other?

While there is no one right answer of what to do in a complicated situation, in general, in such a case, it is better to deal with your angry, insulted feelings and find a constructive way to respond. Today, so many people don't do this. Instead, they act impulsively from emotion before their rational controls kick in, resulting in the everyday carnage that often makes the news, such as in cases of road rage, airline rage, and other sudden angry eruptions that turn into tragedies leading to lost or ruined lives.

The same act-in-haste, regret-it-later effect can occur even in day-to-day angry encounters. And the problem with trying to respond anonymously in today's information age is such actions tend not to stay anonymous very long. Once someone investigates, the incident that led to your anger is likely to come up, leading to a focus on you that reveals what you did.

Thus, instead of seeking revenge, a good approach in a situation where you feel someone has wronged you is to wait until your initial feelings of anger have subsided. Then, if possible, call or write that person and ask to have a discussion with him or her, preferably one-on-one. If he or she agrees, have a heart-to-heart discussion in which you dispassionately describe what happened and how you felt, with a view to improving your relationship in the future. It's an ideal approach with a peer or subordinate to clear the air. If the offending party is your boss, such a discussion may work if he or she is open to such airings of feelings. But otherwise, if you want to stay on the job, it's best to suck up your anger and let it go, or find a way to transform it into doing something productive and profitable.

In short, sweet revenge often is sweet only for a short time, and the long-term effects can turn out to be very sour indeed, when your efforts to seek revenge backfire on you.

# Today's Take-Aways:

 Sweet revenge is often not sweet at all; instead it is often sour and leaves a very bitter taste.

 The problem with seeking revenge is that it often ends up seeking you—or you might fan the flames that end up burning you.

 Once you let go of the anger that's fueling your revenge, you can better think through your options and what it's really best to do.

# 2
## Watch Out *for* *the* Eggshells

With some people you feel like you're walking on eggshells. Often they're very creative, dramatic, or outgoing, and can be very charming and fun to be with. They can be great idea people, enthusiastic salespeople, and dynamic bosses. But they are also very sensitive to potential slights, and they can erupt into tirades or a sullen silence if you say or do the wrong thing to set them off. The experience is like working with a Roman candle that has a short fuse. Or you feel like you are walking through a field of eggshells, and breaking one can be especially dangerous if the problem is with a boss, client, or project team leader.

That's what happened to Andy, an advertising account manager, when he worked with Cynthia, a VP and product manager for an important client. Things could be going along swimmingly, but suddenly, he would get on Cynthia's nerves, and she would erupt and let him have it. At first, Andy wasn't sure exactly what he did to set her off, though he desperately wanted to avoid doing whatever it was, because he was concerned his agency might lose the account or maybe he might get canned himself.

One time an eruption occurred when he was going over billing with Cynthia, at a time when her company had a long-term outstanding debt to the agency that it was gradually paying off. After Andy described the number of hours on the project that his agency would be billing Cynthia's company, Cynthia said "Fine." However, when Andy added: "When?" as in: "When will we get paid?," his remark led to an angry explosion. At first Cynthia told him reassuringly: "Don't worry. You'll get your money." But moments later, she called him back, telling him angrily: "Do you know how insensitive you were to bring up the subject?" Andy spent the next few minutes apologizing and explaining how he hadn't intended to insult her with his question.

Another time, Andy asked Cynthia if she was sure about some facts she was giving him, since he had heard conflicting information. Suddenly she froze up and glared at him. Andy felt she might explode at him in those few seconds, before she turned away, changed the subject, and continued on as if he hadn't said anything to upset her. Afterwards, though, Andy felt an icy reserve in Cynthia's manner toward him at the next few planning meetings he attended with project teams from each company to strategize marketing her product.

Then, one day when Andy needed some information and Cynthia was out of the office, he called someone else in her company for this information. A few days later, when he was on the phone with Cynthia and mentioned how he had already gotten the data from her associate, Cynthia erupted again, accusing him of going around her rather than waiting to speak to her. Another time when Andy told Cynthia about all the things his agency was doing to help her, thinking she would be very appreciative, she instead got very angry. Accusingly, she retorted: "Are you trying to guilt-trip me?" and he felt his efforts to garner appreciation had only backfired.

Andy was becoming more and more uncomfortable about working with Cynthia, yet he wasn't sure what to do, since she was his agency's client. As a result, the increasingly tense situation dragged on, while Andy feared it could easily blow up at any moment, like a smoldering volcano.

Unfortunately, Andy's story is an all too common example of problems in dealing with certain types of supersensitive people. Their emotions are right on the surface, ready to be rubbed raw at the slightest touch that brushes them the wrong way or presses too hard. They are like thin eggshells, ready to break.

# What Should Andy Do?

Here are some possibilities. In Andy's place, what would you do and why? What do you think the outcomes of these different options would be?

 Compliment Cynthia to build up her self-esteem and make her feel better, since she feels insecure. Once she feels more secure, she'll behave better toward you.

 Avoid touching the hot buttons that set Cynthia off by noticing when she starts to become tenser. Then, back off to give her more space to relax and calm down.

 Find a way to not have to deal with Cynthia, say by working around her, such as with a co-worker or her boss.

 Play by the company rules to do everything right. Then, confront her when she acts badly; it's time she grew up.

 Communicate as much as possible by e-mail or memo to reduce the time you need to talk to or meet with Cynthia in person.

 Other?

What should you do if you have to work with this type of individual? One approach is to notice the patterns—what types of questions, comments, or actions set them off? In Cynthia's case, she was very sensitive around money issues that showed how her own company was struggling. She also reacted defensively to any comment that questioned her authority or knowledge or suggested that she was needy. Why should she be so sensitive? The reason is that these were topics that ate at her sense of self-worth and self-assurance. They made her feel insecure and that set her off.

Once you notice these sensitivity patterns in someone, avoid saying or doing what triggers a defensive reaction. Instead, say or do things to build up the person's self-esteem, since that's at the root of the supersensitive response. For instance, instead of seeking Cynthia's appreciation for what his agency was doing for her and her company, making her feel needy, Andy might find ways to compliment her and her company for their contributions. Likewise, if you are working with someone who is apt to explode at the press of a wrong trigger, look for ways to keep from pushing that trigger. Seek to avoid igniting that spark or search for ways to dampen the powder, so it won't go off.

# Today's Take-Aways:

 If you feel like you continually have to walk on eggshells around someone, maybe you should be walking away.

 If you have to stay around someone and feel you are walking on eggshells, find ways to handle the eggs—and that person—more gently so the shells don't break.

 If you find yourself in a box of eggshells—say with a group of supersensitive people—then be light on your feet, so you don't shake up and shatter the eggs.

 If you do break the eggs, try making an omelet. In other words, try to find a soft, gentle way to make repairs in the relationship to smooth things over by building up the person's self-esteem, which may have been shattered like the egg.

# 3
## Don't Fight— Find Out!

Sometimes office fights—much like fights anywhere—can start with deeply held opinions about how things are or should be. The trigger doesn't even have to be something as big as politics. A battle can erupt over ordinary views about what happens every day. As people express their views, they can end up in warring camps, each thinking the other is myopic, even crass, ignorant, and biased. Not surprisingly, workplace relationships can deteriorate from there—interfering with work and productivity. Yet, ironically, such passionately held views are often based on wrong assumptions, premises, and beliefs, so people may not be that far apart after all once these errors are revealed. In fact, sometimes the falling out is due to a communication problem rather than genuine disagreement.

That's what happened in one office lunch room when Sonia described a new product she had heard about—self-stick note pads preprinted with English and Spanish lines of copy about how to clean a house. This way an employer who didn't speak Spanish could post the instructions on a wall or on the refrigerator to tell a non-English-speaking Hispanic employee what to do when he or she came to clean. There were translations for phrases like "Scrub the toilet," "Wash the floors," and "Clean the carpets."

As Sonia described the product, she spoke in increasingly heated, offended tones. "It's racist and offensive," she exclaimed, and pointed out how the product supported the worst stereotypes of "dumb and stupid Mexicans." She continued on, deriding the arrogance of the rich employers who would buy such a product because they don't want to talk to their help. Worse, they probably exploited and underpaid their employees, considering them just lowly servants. Now this product served to demean their employees even more. Soon several other employees discussing the topic in the lunchroom agreed. This was definitely a repulsive, insulting, humiliating product—and another example of how the upper socioeconomic class further put down the servant, lower class in America.

At this point, another employee, Harriet, spoke up and said she thought the product would be helpful and not demeaning at all. She thought the self-stick notes would help an employer explain what he or she wanted, and she described how she had her own team of housekeepers, who were led by a woman who spoke English and came with one or two women from Mexico who spoke only Spanish. "If the owner can't come, I think this would be a great way to communicate with these other women," Harriet said. Then, another employee, Jack, came to her support, saying that he liked the idea too, since he hired household help and would never get his place clean if he didn't hire them. Another woman added that she didn't think it was demeaning to have someone clean a house. "It's like hiring any service, like bringing in someone to fix my computer when it breaks down."

The argument went on, one side stressing the practicality of the product and viewing the others as misguided protectors, and the other side accusing those who liked the product of being myopic, biased, and part of the problem. Over the next week, relationships at work were very strained as a result of the dispute.

The irony of this story is that not one of these employees was Hispanic; they had no idea how people who were Hispanic, worked as housekeepers, and were given self-stick instructions might feel. Instead, the employees each built up their own side of the argument based on their premises and assumptions about other people's feelings and intentions—

in this case, how the housekeepers would feel and how their employers regarded their housekeepers.

# What Should Sonia Have Done?

Here are some possibilities. In Sonia's place, what would you do and why? What do you think the outcomes of these different options would be?

 Sonia was right in expressing her views. Even if the Mexican employees didn't think they were being stereotyped and demeaned, they were.

 Sonia should have found out what the employees who she thought were being demeaned really thought before making her claims; she could have talked to a few employees to find out.

 Sonia should have raised the issue in a neutral way to draw out everyone's opinions before coming to her own conclusions or expressing her opinions so forcefully.

 Sonia shouldn't have raised such a controversial and potentially divisive issue in the workplace in the first place, since it threatens employee relationships and morale.

 Other?

The point of this story is not to say who is right or wrong, but to show how mistaken we can be when we make assumptions about what people think and feel. Such assumptions can be especially dangerous in a multicultural environment, where people come from many different perspectives. Thus, rather than imagining how people might react to some situation, it is better to ask and find out.

That's what Harriet did a few weeks later, when her Russian housekeeper, Elva, who was married to a man from El Salvador, arrived with two Spanish-speaking women to clean her house. Harriet described the debate at work to Elva, who said she didn't find the notes offensive. Then, Elva translated Harriet's question into Spanish and asked her employees, who responded in Spanish, and Elva translated their answers for Harriet. "No, they say they wouldn't think it's insulting at all if an employer left them these notes. They say it would be helpful. They would like to know what their employer wants them to do."

Harriet had her answer. She found out for sure rather than continuing to rely on her assumptions of what her housekeepers might think and feel. So now she knew should this subject come up again at work—although in this case, she decided not to bring up the subject herself, since people had stopped talking about the topic and relationships had improved. She didn't want to risk disrupting the relationships again, though she was ready to give her informed opinion if someone else brought up the topic.

Likewise, if you're in a situation in which people have developed opinions about what others think and believe, ask yourself whether they really know what they are talking about, or whether you do yourself. Or is the debate and disagreement fueled by untested premises, assumptions, and beliefs about the facts? If so, don't keep holding on to your own unsupported opinion. Instead, find out what the facts really are. This way, your opinion, whatever it is, will be based on what you know. Then, too, when everyone has the true facts, often the source of disagreement can wither away. In fact, sometimes everyone may turn out to share similar opinions, once they see the true picture.

# Today's Take-Aways:

 If you're fighting about the facts, sometimes that's because you and others don't know what the facts really are.

Don't just imagine or assume what the facts must be; find out when you don't know or aren't sure.

 Sometimes firmly held opinions are inversely related to what people really know; if so, seek to reverse the equation by providing them with the facts.

# 4

# When *to* Turn Down *the* Volume, *or* Find Someone Else *to* Do It

Sometimes simmering workplace feuds can bubble along under the surface. You know they are there, because of a sense of unspoken tension between two or more people who work together. But often such low-level tensions are ignored in the interest of keeping the peace. In some cases, such feuds start off being one sided, when one person is offended by or simply doesn't like another employee and shows this in subtle ways. Some common methods include quiet putdowns; indirect insults; or passive–aggressive tactics, such as agreeing to take on certain responsibilities for a joint assignment and not doing them properly or at all, so the disliked person ends up looking bad. As such guerrilla hostilities continue, the victim is likely to strike back, perhaps by some undercover action, too. An unspoken feud can easily escalate and heat up, creating a truly steamy brew that can explode and spread to others.

That's what happened to Betty, an office manager who handled program planning at a health service. She wasn't sure exactly how the problem started, but she noticed that the administrative assistant, Allison, who was supposed to help coordinate her meetings and trainings, seemed to have some kind of gripe against her. Betty felt this way because of how Allison reacted on numerous occasions. Allison repeatedly sounded annoyed when Betty asked her to provide the material she needed for a presentation. Allison made several easily avoidable mistakes in getting requested equipment. At meetings, Allison offered subtle putdowns, suggesting Betty wasn't competent, with remarks such as: "Didn't you hear me when I told you three times?"

At first, Betty attributed Allison's actions to her simply having a bad day. But as the actions added up, Betty saw a pattern, as if she were the target of an office sniper. For instance, one time Betty needed a laptop computer and projector for a PowerPoint presentation. When Betty made her request, Allison sounded hesitant, at which point Betty offered to go directly to the equipment department. Allison quickly responded defensively: "No, don't do it. I'll take care of it," as if Betty was threatening to usurp her authority in taking care of getting the equipment herself. Then at the meeting, though Allison brought the equipment, she hadn't learned how to set it up, and when Betty offered to try to do so, Allison refused to let her try if she hadn't done this before. "I'm responsible for the equipment," she said. The result was that Betty couldn't use the equipment for her training program. Another time, Betty didn't hear what Allison said at a meeting, and when Betty asked Allison to repeat it, Allison jumped on her, accusing her of being rude for not listening.

The culminating incident came a few weeks later, at the end of a meeting. Betty was uncertain about what another employee's responsibilities were after the woman resigned from a position, and a new person agreed to take over some of her responsibilities. But it wasn't clear to Betty who was doing what now, and when she asked for clarification, Allison snapped at her: "Oh, weren't you at that meeting?" Though Betty let the remark pass without an immediate response, she was clearly hurt, and as she added up the dozens of remarks and actions by Allison over the last two months, she felt something was clearly wrong. But she wasn't sure what the problem was and wasn't sure what to do. Continue to ignore such behavior and hope for the best? Confront Allison privately to bring her motivation out in the open? Raise the problem for discussion at a meeting where she might gain support? Fight back covertly to put Allison on notice that she wasn't going to take her rude insults and actions anymore? Or what?

# What Should Betty Do?

Here are some possibilities. In Betty's place, what would you do and why? What do you think the outcomes of these different options would be?

 Ignore Allison's putdowns, mistakes, and lack of responsive behavior; think of them as Allison's problem rather than taking them personally, and hope things will get smoothed over if you don't stir up the pot.

 Arrange for a private meeting with Allison and ask her what the problem is and what you can do to help resolve whatever's bothering her.

 Bring up her experiences at a staff meeting to alert others to the problem, gain their support, and prevent Allison from continuing to get away with her actions.

 Find a way to undermine Allison quietly and expose her bad behavior to others, so maybe she'll lose her job.

 Find a co-worker on good terms with Allison to step in, find out what the problem is, and try to work things out between you.

 Other?

Resolving such conflicts can be tricky, because you are dealing with covert and indirect behavior, like the low-volume static on a radio playing in the background. As the volume increases, it is more likely to attract attention; and if you don't take action, the volume will get louder and louder, and the noise can increasingly interfere with good working relationships. The process is much like what happens when a bubbling kettle heats up until it finally explodes, if you don't let out the steam. Worse, as a toxic relationship continues, it not only harms the original parties, but can also negatively affect everyone in the office with its poisonous fumes.

Thus, when such a problem continues for a while, find a way to "turn down the volume," just as you might release steam from an overheated kettle. But should you be the one to do it? At times a direct conversation is the best approach. You ask the other person if you did anything to offend him or her and have a productive discussion to clear the air. Sometimes, particularly when the other person is being furtive, it's better to bring in a neutral third party, especially someone who knows you both.

For instance, if Betty were to contact Allison directly, Allison might immediately get defensive, deny she did anything to hurt or insult Betty, or perhaps argue and hurl back even more insults, escalating the problem still further. By contrast, a neutral third party who is already friends with Allison might be just the antidote to start the healing process and set the stage for a frank discussion promoting reconciliation. The neutral third party might be better able to do this, since Allison might feel safe enough to air her feelings and reasons for her actions, without thinking she has to protect herself from someone she already feels negative about. Then, after an opening discussion gets the reasons for the problem on the table, the neutral third party can act as a mediator, helping to find a resolution by bringing the parties in conflict together and generally clearing the air.

In this case, that's exactly what Betty did. She called Ben, a colleague who knew them both, and described the escalating series of events that led her to feel Allison was upset about something she might have done. As it turned out, Allison had imagined some offhand comment of Betty's showed a lack of respect for her, and rather than saying anything to clear the air, had continued to feel quietly angry. After Ben reassured Betty that he hadn't noticed anything offensive about Betty's own behavior, he said he would talk to Allison, which he did, helping to set the stage for a peaceful resolution.

In sum, as a workplace feud starts to build, turn down the volume before it becomes too loud. At the same time, consider if you are the one to do this, or if it may be best to have someone else help you do it.

# Today's Take-Aways:

 To turn down the volume on a conflict, sometimes it's better to have someone do it for you.

 Just like you get rid of static on the radio to get a clear channel, in a conflict, bringing things out in the open can promote clarity and get rid of the noise.

 If you sense that someone is acting covertly against you, that's like detecting low-level static on the radio. Seek to eliminate the problem as soon as possible, so the channel—and the relationship—becomes clear again.

 Remember that people have their own receptions—like those on a radio—and tune in to different levels, so that some people are more sensitive than others. What one person means as a quiet joking comment can sound like a loud hurtful insult to the other. If so, it's time to turn down the volume on that broadcast, too.

# 5

# When *a* Problem Spirals Out *of* Control

If conflicts at work mushroom, feuds can turn into vendettas and spiral far beyond the original problem. Even some attempts to resolve them can backfire, as the blame game creates more and more victims. In such cases, even if you are not at fault, it is best to deal with blame and false allegations in a calm, cool, strategic way, or risk being caught in the undertow.

The situation is like being a passenger in a boat that could be capsized by a crazed passenger who is blaming you for a storm. You didn't cause the storm; you are not in charge of the boat; but the passenger thinks you are. So you have to gain control of the passenger or situation, but do so in a calm, controlled way—or your boat will go down.

That's what happened to one man—let's call him Dan—who wrote to me about an increasingly desperate work situation at his department in a nonprofit agency, which was headed up by two senior employees. Unfortunately, the office was often in turmoil because one problem employee, Tom, often slacked off on his job. He frequently came in late or took extra long lunches, and when he worked, he often made errors that had to be corrected by his colleagues. When one senior employee, Barry, complained to the agency director, the director initiated a meeting with Barry and Tom to discuss Tom's performance. At the meeting,

Tom denied Barry's description of his work habits and argued back that Barry had been picking on him. To solve the problem, the agency director called a meeting a week later with the whole department, which included the letter writer Dan.

During the meeting, Dan offered his own opinions about Tom's poor work habits, confirming Barry's original complaint. The two senior employees who ran the department decided to set up a new work schedule for Tom, so he would put in the required hours and be more productive. But after two days, Dan noticed that Tom was not following this new schedule and was still making many errors, and after Dan reported this to Barry, Barry spoke to Tom. Soon after, Tom said he didn't feel well, and headed home.

But the next day, Tom returned determined to get back at everyone, especially Dan. Within a few hours, Tom announced he was going to file sexual harassment charges against Dan. Though they were untrue, Dan was immediately terrified that in the ensuing investigation, some personal problems he had once confided in Tom would be revealed, since he feared Tom would bring up old skeletons from the past, including a long-buried criminal conviction. In Dan's view, Tom didn't care if his allegations of sexual harassment against Dan weren't true. He just wanted to create as much havoc at work before he finally was fired, including embarrassing Dan by bringing up these old charges in an investigation.

# What Should Dan Do?

Here are some possibilities. What would you do as Dan and why? And what do you think the outcomes of these different options would be?

 Tell a supervisor about Tom's threat to file untrue harassment charges and acknowledge the long-buried criminal conviction in confidence to deal with that now, before it potentially leaks. (This way maybe his supervisor might be more understanding about him concealing this information, though the concealment could be grounds for dismissal.)

Talk to Tom to try to overcome his feeling of resentment and even offer to help, to avoid his filing the charges, even if untrue.

 Wait until Tom actually does something, since it could be an idle threat; then, deal with whatever charges or negative information that come up when they do.

 Find a new job, get a good recommendation, and go, before these problems erupt and you leave with mud on your face.

 Confront Tom and tell him in no uncertain terms how you'll fight back if he files any false charges or releases any private information against you, since you could get damages for defamation or invasion of privacy.

Other?

W hat should Dan do to avoid being dragged down by this runamok employee? A first step would be to find out whether Tom was just making threats and whether his charges were based on some kind of misunderstanding or were completely unjustified and just being used for revenge. Then, if Tom's plan to file charges was still merely a threat, Dan might still have time to talk to Tom and smooth over any problems. Should there be a misunderstanding, perhaps this could be worked through—or even if Tom was contemplating revenge, maybe his anger could be defused. For instance, if he was feeling a lack of respect and understanding, maybe Dan could build Tom up to feel better about himself and less angry with Dan.

Or suppose Tom did already register his sexual harassment complaint with someone else, such as Barry or another employee. Perhaps Dan could talk to this person to learn what the charges were and give his side of the story. In fact, because of privacy considerations, these employees might already be bound to keep the charges confidential, particularly when they were only alleged but unproven, so these other employees could probably be trusted to keep Dan's confidences.

In short, down the road, Dan might have invasion of privacy or other grounds for legal action should private information about him be revealed hurting his reputation. But long before that, my suggestion to him was to try to talk to first Tom and then Barry to work out this conflict in a spirit of understanding and problem solving. In fact, it was best for Dan not to bring up the legal possibilities as threats in his conversations with Dan, unless these other approaches didn't work. (Even then, these might not really be viable options given a hard to win case.) After all, why bring up potential future retaliatory actions if you are trying for harmony and reconciliation now. To talk of retaliation is like holding up a hammer while saying you want to work for peace—a contradiction between what you are saying and doing that usually doesn't work. Moreover, if Tom was already acting like a loose cannon in the office, anything that might make him even more angry and defensive could light the spark to make the cannon go off.

Thus, even though Dan may have done nothing wrong and had only gotten the problem employee furious at him by speaking the truth, he still had to find a way to contain the problem before it spiraled out of control.

Likewise, if you're in a potentially out-of-control situation, think of ways to get it under control. Perhaps imagine the situation like a raging fire, where you want to use water to douse the flames, and want to avoid doing anything to add fuel to the fire. In other words, use sweet talk and words of support and reconciliation to smooth over the relationship; stay away from accusations and threats that might fan the flames. Maybe the senior managers might have kept down the tension by having a discussion about his performance problems with Tom individually rather than at a group meeting where everyone aired their complaints. But then, the complaints were widespread, so they wanted to hash out the problems openly. Once the laundry was out in the open, so to speak, Dan had to deal with the situation; he couldn't control what the senior managers did.

# Today's Take-Aways:

 If you're facing a fired-up employee, a first step is to put out the fire.

 When others are raging, think of ways of engaging.

 Just as honey can make the medicine go down, sweet talk can sometimes be just the medicine to put down office conflicts.

 Avoid threatening legal action when someone's already enraged and upset. These could be fighting words that provoke even more fight from someone ready to go off.

# 6

# Prepare *for the* Worst-Case Scenario

Everyone agrees that preparation is absolutely critical. Whether it's a speaking presentation, a report you are writing, a sales meeting, or something else, preparation is a major key to success. Usually when people talk about preparation, they are talking about follow-up; perseverance; getting the facts; doing the research needed; and practice, practice, practice. But even if you do all of these things and feel fully prepared, are you really?

Unfortunately, you can be perfectly well prepared for what you expect. But then you may find you have done all this great preparation and things are not what they seem. You are hit with the unexpected and unpredictable. You encounter the "worst-case scenario" and you didn't consider it a possibility at the time. The experience is a little like spending weeks and weeks preparing for a big exam only to find out that the exam will be on another subject that you haven't prepped for at all. Likewise, in the workplace, you might get all that research data your manager wants, only to discover the company's marketing program has changed, so he wants the research about something else. Or maybe you think you are giving an informal presentation to a small group in your office and are fully prepared for that only to find the arrangements changed. Instead of talking to a small group, you are now one of the featured presenters at the company's upcoming conference.

That's why contingency planning is critical; you can think of alternate possibilities, even fairly unlikely ones, so you are prepared for the unexpected—and are even ready for still other unpredictable possibilities should they occur. In fact, often such unexpected events occur because people don't communicate their expectations clearly in the first place or they later change their minds at the last minute, whether because of changed circumstances or on whim. Even with the best of advance discussion on your part, you may still be left in the dark confronting the unexpected and unknown—a problem compounded when you are dealing with difficult people who are poor communicators or unpredictable themselves. But at least preparation for contingencies can help you shift more quickly and with less pain to Plan B, C, or X, Y, Z.

Otherwise, like Emily, you might be caught short and have to scramble around after the fact to see if you can repair the fallout from not being prepared for the unexpected. Emily was a department manager in a small graphics and Web site design company, and she handled most of the purchasing of outside supplies and services, including from one very large corporation—let's call it ABC Enterprises—which provided the company's software for all of its operations, from product design to accounting.

Everything seemed routine and business-as-usual until Emily's company decided to expand into a larger office suite in the building, and that meant moving their computers and setting them up in another network configuration. When Emily called to arrange for the new system, ABC's salesman, Bert, was only too happy to help with the order, including suggesting a new line of equipment designed to produce even speedier connections in network systems. The price would be a little higher, but Bert persuaded her that the speed and organizing features of the networking software would be worth the extra cost. Thus, after hearing Bart explain how the old system was set up and what would be moved where to create the new linked system, and hearing his assurances that he knew exactly what she needed, she gave him the okay to order the equipment.

That's when problems started that would go on over the next three months. First, some of the technicians who came over had not been fully trained in how to install the new equipment. After spending a couple of hours going through the company's offices, they gave up, unable to install anything, though they left several boxes of equipment they had planned to install. Then, when a trained technician arrived, he discovered that the equipment that the first technicians had left for the installation wasn't the correct type for Emily's company, so they had to order new equipment, resulting in further delays. Meanwhile, the company's operations were seriously hampered, since while awaiting the new software, some equipment had been disconnected from a central network terminal, so information had to be transferred manually from computer to computer.

In short, the process was a big mess, and after about two weeks of mix-ups, Emily decided to start carefully documenting what happened, along with calculating the time lost and expenses incurred. She also sent copies to the managers at ABC Enterprises, and after four weeks, when the software system still wasn't installed because of more delays due to sending equipment to the wrong address, she got another salesman, Jerry, to work on straightening out the orders and getting it right. Even Jerry's manager, Tony, had to intervene to help in untangling the past order information and figuring out what Emily's company really needed to link up all their systems and integrate them with the new software.

Afterwards, Emily began the process of getting compensation for her company's losses and damages, turning first to the company's own insurance company, and then asking Tony at ABC to help her file a claim. But now after being so helpful, Tony said he couldn't do anything more to assist and referred her to ABC's CEO, who passed her claim on to the company's risk management division, which promptly lost her claim for a month. After they found it, they were slow to respond, finally sending her a letter that said in essence, "We're sorry but we are responsible only for replacing any faulty equipment."

Eventually, after more fruitless attempts to contact a high-up ABC official to work out a settlement, Emily gave up. She decided to take the matter to small claims court and divide up the claim to cover the different types of delays and damage caused by different technicians. At least, the compensation might provide some small consolation, and she figured that if she showed she was serious by filing a suit, ABC would come around and offer a settlement. After all, she reasoned, it would be costly for any of their executives to prepare a case and come to court from their headquarters, about one and a half hours away by car. But when no settlement offer was forthcoming, she figured she'd have to go to court.

If it came to that, at least she would be carefully prepared. She gathered documents showing a paper trail of wrong deliveries, assembled a chronology of the many problems and delays caused by the untrained technicians and delivery of wrong equipment, and even collected examples of other individuals and companies who complained about their problems with ABC. She used the Internet to do much of her research, and also articles about the company from the local paper. In addition, she found a news group where many participants complained about ABC Enterprises, and downloaded records of several successful suits against them that had been posted on-line. In her view, the case was a fairly straightforward one, with no dispute about the facts. After all, she figured, besides the long paper trail of documents, she had a detailed chronology of events that Tony and others at ABC had already seen, without raising any questions about its accuracy.

Thus, when it finally came time to go to court, Emily felt very confident she was fully prepared. She even thought her binder with all the documents, table of contents, and list of major points in her case would be compelling, particularly when she saw the slim file folders that Tony from ABC brought with him to court. As a result, in giving her presentation, she handed her big binder to the judge, but rather than walk the judge through her detailed chronology, since small claims presentations are usually limited to a few minutes and she expected no dispute about facts, she presented a broad overview. She touched briefly on how she repeatedly encountered untrained technicians or technicians with the wrong equipment, then focused on what she thought would be the hardest to prove—the number of hours her company lost and the hours she spent dealing with the problem. This way she could turn the hours spent and lost multiplied by what she usually earned per hour into a total amount of compensation requested for damages.

When it was time for Tony to respond, he read from a written statement in which he disputed her account of events date by date; attributed many statements to her that she was certain she did not say; and spoke with such anger and hostility toward her that she was floored. Before Tony had been so helpful in trying to help her sort things out. But now he hit her hard with his accusations, arguing that she was confused and caused her own installation delays by not knowing what was in her system and what was needed. Date by date, he went down his list, quoting statements she had made, even prefacing some with the comment: "and that's in her own words." But the words hadn't been hers. Again and again, his statements, spoken with such authority, contradicted her own chronology. What hurt even more was his summary conclusion: "So you can see, Ms. Anthony has simply brought these two cases to cover up her own confusion in placing the incorrect orders, which is what caused all of these delays and her company's losses. Instead, she has sued us to get us to pay for her own mistakes and to get our software system at no charge."

When he concluded, after 15 minutes of reading his prepared statement like a prosecutor in a criminal case, she felt so stunned that she could barely reply, except to say she felt floored and didn't know how to answer his response, which she said sounded like fiction. "He made so many false accusations. I don't know where to begin. And I didn't go through my own detailed chronology, because I thought there wouldn't be any question about the basic facts."

But obviously there was such a question, and since Emily had only heard Tony's statements and now saw the judge looking at her with glazed eyes after Tony's long detailed reading, she felt he wouldn't be receptive to another detailed presentation. Besides she felt drained and defeated, so she ended by simply saying: "I wasn't confused. You'll see in my chronology how the first salesman kept getting it wrong."

Yet, would the judge ever see this? While the judge scooped up her binder with her chronology and Tony's thin file, saying: "I'll take the case under submission," she wondered if he would actually read her chronology or give it proper consideration. After all, Tony's presentation had been so forceful and damning. And all his lies. She certainly hadn't expected or been prepared for that, since he had once been so helpful. Yet now he had turned on her like a pit viper, spewing poison. It was only after she left the courtroom that Emily began to realize that she had been blindsided by Tony's lies about her, which questioned her honesty, motives, and integrity in even bringing the case.

# What Should Emily Have Done and What Should She Do Now?

Here are some possibilities. In Emily's place, what would you have done or do now and why? What do you think the outcomes of these different options would be?

 Try to talk to Tony, as well as ABC's risk management department, to work out a settlement, if he has the authority to participate in the process.

 Look at the mix-ups that happened from Tony's point of view to consider how he and ABC might try to get out of taking the blame.

 Document not only what happened to show delays and damage but document your conversations with Tony and others in ABC.

 Besides writing a letter to the judge about Tony's lies, share this information with the media, since this could be a big story involving a big company. At least you would feel you gained justice, whatever happens at court.

 Send a complaint letter about Tony and ABC to various regulatory agencies; maybe they'll take action against ABC.

 Other?

T hus, while Emily had prepared carefully, she had never contemplated the possibility that Tony might question her version of the facts or that he might lie to protect ABC from any liability. She was in fact fully prepared—but not for the right thing, not for the unpredictable.

She had been so certain the case would go one way, and when it turned into something else, she didn't know how to respond to that.

Instead, Emily should have carefully checked her assumptions about the basis of her case and the possible counter-arguments that might be used against her. Then, too, she shouldn't have been so trusting that Tony was the nice guy he seemed, since he was nice when trying to help her correct a problem his own company had caused and reduce any potential damage claims. But once Emily filed suit again ABC and his company refused responsibility for any damages, he became the opposition. Now the situation was different, and Emily should have considered that his attitude toward her might change along with his role. Though the judge did actually take the time to read Emily's materials and she did win the case, she spent an agonizing two months waiting and worrying about how she had probably lost the case. In many small claims cases, a judge might decide the case on the spot without reading anything.

By the same token, when you're facing a challenge such as going to court or doing anything that involves substantial preparation, consider what you are preparing for. Check out any assumptions. Engage in scenario thinking, where you consider different possibilities. Ask yourself "what if" questions, think about how you might respond under different situations, and prepare accordingly, so you are ready if the situation changes. Such thinking of different possibilities will also help you be more nimble on your feet generally, because you will have already considered the unexpected and unpredictable. You will be more able to adapt whatever the circumstances.

But what if you haven't prepared properly for the unpredictable? Is there anything you can do now? Well, maybe there is if you do some creative thinking and shift your preparation in another direction.

# Today's Take-Aways:

 When you least expect it, the unexpected will occur; so prepare for the unexpected in case you don't get what you expect.

ıen situations change, so can people; so be prepared for
ople to change their attitudes and their actions when they
e placed in different situations and play different roles.

 Your preparations are only as good as your predictions, and sometimes your predictions can be wrong. So prepare for the unpredictable, too.

 Just because you know things happened a certain way doesn't mean that others know that or want things to be that way. So be prepared that someone else may tell a different story, whether he believes it or just wants others to believe his point of view.

 Don't expect people always to tell the truth, even in court. If there's an incentive to lie and a good chance of not getting caught, people often will—so be prepared for that, too.

# When Nothing Is *the* Best Solution

W hile everyone talks about being "proactive" as a good strategy, whether you're solving a problem or planning for the future, sometimes the best strategy is to do nothing and wait, even when you are eager to do something, anything. That's because taking no action can seem so powerless; yet at times the power comes in your ability to wait and let someone else make his or her move first.

That's what happened to Joe, when his company hired a local software designer, Aaron. The plan was to create a dedicated Web site to market some specialty educational toys that Joe's company had been selling locally through department stores and trade shows. Joe had been thinking of going online for some time but didn't have the knowledge to set up a commercial site himself, despite a few introductory classes on creating Web pages. Thus, he was delighted when he ran into Aaron at a local business networking meeting, and Aaron described his skills. Definitely, he sounded like the "can do everything person" Joe needed, from setting up the site to processing and sending out the orders. Joe would just have to supply the products, photos to use on the site, promotional copy, and some leads for potential buyers. "And I'll do the rest," Aaron assured him. "Besides, I'm an expert in Internet marketing."

But since Joe didn't have the revenue to pay Aaron a decent salary, Aaron agreed to work on a commission basis such that they would share proceeds 50–50 after expenses. Though it was understood that Aaron was still doing his own work for other clients, he would spend a substantial amount of time working for Joe.

For the first month or two, things seemed to be going well, or at least Joe thought they were. He submitted a few ideas for the Web site layout and design to Aaron, who fine-tuned them and set up the site, using Joe's copy and photos. He also began taking some lists of organizations of educators and parents that Joe had gathered to put them into databases, though he complained they weren't in the right format, so it was taking him longer than expected. Meanwhile, as Aaron spent more time, as he claimed, working on these databases, Joe began to do more on creating the pages for the Web site than he had expected, using the first few pages as a template. After a few weeks, some online orders began to dribble in, mainly from people who saw the flyers that Joe used when he showed off the product line at events and from their friends. Then, as agreed, Aaron mailed out the orders, and Joe kept track of the sales, which showed that the partnership was slowly approaching the break-even point.

But soon, signs of problems developed. First, when profits were slow to come in, Aaron said he had to place his first priority on other paying work, though he agreed to spend about 15 hours a week on the project. A few weeks after that, Aaron said he was sick and wasn't able to spend more than a few hours a week on the project, mostly to send out the few orders that Joe brought in. At first, Joe was very sympathetic, wishing Aaron the best for a speedy recovery, and he agreeably took on more of the Web design tasks. When Aaron expressed some guilt that he wasn't pulling his own weight on the project, Joe simply reassured him that he enjoyed doing the work on the Web site and not to worry. "Just get well."

Over the next few weeks, as Aaron's illness dragged on, Joe began to do some of the work on the databases, and that's when he discovered that Aaron had made all kinds of mistakes in setting up the data fields and entering data. Also, some of the special pages that Aaron had set up for processing and tracking orders didn't work right. In short, not only was Aaron not doing much of the work because of his illness, but Joe also realized that Aaron didn't know as much as he claimed about some things.

Now, Joe felt, with a little additional work the online site seemed to be on the verge of breaking even and taking off. So all he needed was someone else to do this work. Yet, could he, should he, do this?

# What Should Joe Do?

Here are some possibilities. In Joe's place, what would you have done and why? What do you think the outcomes of these different options would be?

 Tell Aaron after he has been ill for a couple of weeks that he hasn't been pulling his share, and though you are sympathetic, you have to get someone else to do the work if he can't.

 Fill in for Aaron because he is sick, but confront him when you discover his many mistakes, since he has misrepresented his abilities and doesn't deserve to continue to work on the project for that reason.

 Continue to let Aaron think you will be ready for him to come back to the business when he is well; but meanwhile, look for a new employee to do his work, and be ready to compensate Aaron for his time, should the business take off with the new employee.

 Show Aaron great sympathy in his illness, but explain that the business is doing poorly without him, can't be saved, and let him be the one to accept this reality and decide to leave himself and relinquish any copyright claims in return for a small payment.

 Other?

Unfortunately, this is one of those times when the answer was not straightforward, because even if Joe had discovered the employee he hired wasn't pulling his weight, his employee could potentially have a copyright claim on what he had contributed. He hadn't been paid in cash, as in a usual work for hire arrangement, but instead there was a percentage agreement. The problem could become especially sticky if the sales and profits at the Web site took off. So what Joe really needed first was a way to get Aaron to agree he had no copyright claims on what he had contributed. But how?

The best way was literally to stop doing anything to make the Web site successful in order to show Aaron that the business was doomed to fail. Maybe he should do enough to handle the occasional sale that came in himself, but otherwise do nothing to promote it. This way, when Aaron was ready to return to work on the project, he might think it was a lost cause and agree to drop any further claims in exchange for a small payment, leaving Joe free to find another employee without worrying about potential claims from a previous one. Or maybe from what he learned in the interim while Aaron was ill he might not even need to hire someone else. Maybe he could run the business himself and hire some assistants when needed as the business took off.

To use the phrase of one of my associates, this was the time to "Put the dog on the porch." It was an expression he had learned from his grandfather in Texas, and it meant that sometimes when your dog misbehaved, it was time to put it out on the porch and feed it from time to time. But otherwise, "Leave the dog out there until you are ready to let him back in."

Likewise, here, Joe should put his business on the porch for awhile to keep it alive, but not pay much attention to it, so that his former employee would lose interest and move on without making a copyright or other claim for anything he might have contributed, even if minimal. That's what Joe did. At the same time, instead of sending Aaron updates on what he had been doing to keep the business going and calling Aaron every few days to wish him well, he simply stopped calling. Let Aaron be the one to show an interest in what was happening in the business, and the longer it took for Aaron to do anything, the better it was. It indicated that Aaron was abandoning his interest in the business, and after a month or two, if Aaron didn't state so himself, Joe could take some steps to clarify the end of their working arrangement and any claims Aaron might have. For example, he might send a letter describing how the business had not been successful, and offering Aaron a small payment for what he did contribute in return for a note from Aaron indicating that he no longer had any interest in or claims on the business.

By the same token, if you are in a situation where you want to end a work relationship and want to make sure the other party has no unjustified claims on it, you are in a better position if you let him or her make the move to end the relationship, rather than proactively seeking to end it yourself. Certainly, if you have a short time frame for resolving the situation, you may not be able to do this. But if you can, wait it out by "putting the dog on the porch." Do what you need to keep the dog alive; but otherwise, don't invite the dog back in. Rather, let the dog show it's ready to behave before you open the door to let it come inside. That way you stay in better control of the situation; your power comes from waiting and doing nothing. For then, a dog that isn't ready to behave will simply go away, much as Joe hoped Aaron would do, and Aaron eventually did. By contrast, if you try to confront or discipline the dog too soon, he may bite and fight back. Better to let him leave on his own if you decide you don't want him back in the house.

# Today's Take-Aways:

 When you aren't sure what to do, the best strategy may be to simply wait.

 There can be great power and wisdom in doing nothing, because action or resistance might provoke a counter-response.

 Instead of escalating the action to end a situation, try waiting it out to see if it will end on its own.

 Sometimes it's best to treat a situation like a dog on the porch. Put it away for awhile, give it minimal attention, and it'll eventually either work itself out (ie: behave) or simply wind down (ie: go away).

# 8
## Keep It Clear, Clear, Clear

Communication breakdowns are at the heart of so many conflicts and foul-ups. They can occur at every stage of a communication from sender to recipient and back again. From wrong assumptions to wrong information that shapes a message to misunderstandings and misinterpretations when you "get"—or maybe don't "get"—it, the possibilities for mix-ups are endless. How can you increase the chances of getting a clear message across? How can you know if that clear message has been received?

That's the problem Trina faced when she was assigned an eager but not always on-task employee—Steven—to manage on her project team. His job was to gather the research findings about the company's marketing efforts in different cities, analyze them, turn them into charts and presentations, and send them to the clients. Others on the team were involved in doing interviews or collecting survey data and turning the results in to Steven. Part of Trina's job was to give Steven guidelines on the priorities for different projects, so he could meet company timelines. However, after she gave Steven instructions, usually by e-mail, phone, or in a personal meeting, he frequently got the instructions wrong. Sometimes he changed her instructions to set up the research analysis or reports in different ways, because he thought these were better, though Trina did not. Sometimes he spent what Trina considered an excessive amount of time trying out different ways to set up the data, saying he was looking for greater efficiencies, when Trina felt he was simply wasting time.

Trina also objected to Steven's seeming arrogance in claiming he had certain research skills, when Trina had her doubts that he did. Compounding the problem, he often became defensive when she pointed out a mistake, so she felt she had to be especially diplomatic to protect his feelings. While she felt mistakes were an ordinary part of learning to improve, Steven reacted to any suggestion he had made a mistake with a wall of resistance, as if admitting any mistake would challenge the air of invincible expertise he tried to maintain. For instance, once when she told him she hadn't received a copy of several reports he sent to the client, he bristled: "But I did send them. You always get a copy; it's in the program." So Trina backed down as she commonly did, quietly telling him to print another copy for her or send it again.

Yet as much as she wished she could fire Steven, Trina felt she couldn't, because he had a fairly secure lock on the job, much like a civil service "no-termination without cause" position. So Trina thought her only option was trying to get him to perform better without raising his defenses. But how?

# What Should Trina Do?

Here are some possibilities. In Trina's place, what would you have done or do now and why? What do you think the outcomes of these different options would be?

 Find a way to get Steven fired. Why spend the extra time trying to make things clear to him, if it's hard for him to understand?

 Give Steven a clear set of written instructions, but tell him his job is on the line if he doesn't finally get it right. Even if it may be difficult to fire him, the warning alone might scare him into paying more attention, so he will do the work right.

Have a team meeting for everyone to discuss what Steven is doing wrong, so he really gets the message. By using the group meeting, you won't be alone in having problems with his work, as the difficulties will now concern everyone on the team.

 Take some private time to explain the problem to Steven, find out from him what he suggests to solve it, and use those insights to help you make future projects and priorities clear to him using multiple channels of information.

 Other?

My advice to Trina was twofold. First, maybe Steven didn't fully understand her instructions the first time she told him what to do. Thus, she might try communicating with him through multiple channels and at different times, so he would be more likely to get the message, yet not think she was repeating it exactly, which might seem like an insult. For instance, if she gave the original instruction in an e-mail or phone conversation, she might repeat it again at a face-to-face meeting and follow up with a memo that would go to him and others working on the project, outlining what everyone was supposed to do. Or if she sent out a memo with instructions, she might follow up with a phone call or face-to-face meeting to see if he got the memo and fully understood it. Such follow-up involved more work for her, but it would provide more assurance that Steven would get her instructions right.

Second, given Steven's defensiveness, it might help to reassure him to meet with him personally to find out what he felt he needed to do to better give the client what he wanted. To provide him with more motivation, it might help to have Steven meet with her and the client or have a three-way phone conversation with her and the client, so he felt like he was doing the work for the client, not just for her.

And that's what Trina did. First, she set up a meeting with Steven and gently described some of the problems, such as the unmet deadlines and unreceived reports. She concluded by asking: "So what can I do to help you? What kind of barriers are standing in the way that I can help to get out of the way?"

Steven appreciated the questions. He felt Trina was treating him as an equal colleague rather than giving him orders, and he responded in kind. "Well, sometimes I do forget what I'm supposed to be doing, when I get things to do assigned to me at different times. And I'm not always sure what's most important for me to do first, so I might leave those things to the side if I don't think they're that important and then forget." Finally, he addressed Trina's concerns about his changing report formats and content. "Maybe it would help, too, if I knew why you or the client wanted something laid out in a certain way. Then, I wouldn't try to make any changes. I was just trying to do what I thought was better."

The meeting helped to clear the air as well as overcome an underlying source of the problem—Steven's unconscious resistance to being told what to do by Trina, because he resented her authority. But now that she had explained the needs of the project and presented herself as more of a facilitator than his boss, he felt more comfortable and less threatened.

Trina also devoted more time to writing up clearly what she wanted, too, after the meeting. She wrote more detailed memos in which she laid out more clearly, in step-by-step fashion, what should be done, and to illustrate, included examples of formatting and styles to use, so it was absolutely clear what should be done and in what order. She additionally took time to introduce the memo through alternate means—by e-mail, phone, or through a one-on-one or group meeting. A few days later, she further followed up with Steven to see that he fully understood, agreed with, and could do the tasks assigned to him in time for the next deadline. From time to time, Trina followed up, not to nag, but to see if Steven needed any additional help with the required tasks.

Likewise, if you are working with someone who is not following instructions or getting things wrong, try different strategies to see how you can make what you want done more clear and precise—and do so in a way that won't make someone defensive. Rather than blame, think about how you can help the person get things right. Recognize, too, that some people are more responsive to getting information in different ways. That's why finding different ways to repeat the message can help in a nonthreatening way, so the other person doesn't feel patronized. Even adding humorous cartoons or quotes to a _____ might be a way to add variation and a light touch to help the message go down more easily. In other words, if you combine some: Clarity + Concern + Clarity + Compassion + Clarity, that might help you get your message across in a way that makes the other person more receptive and willing to listen, understand, and respond.

# Today's Take-Aways:

 If something isn't clear one way, try using one or more other channels of communication to reinforce what you want to say.

 Don't just *say* it; find ways to *write* it and *show* it, too.

 Combine a little concern and compassion with clarity to help the clarity go down—just as you might add sugar to medicine or give someone a sugar-coated pill to make it easier to swallow.

 Don't just try to make it clear yourself. Try to get the other person to shine some light, as well, to clear the way.

# PART II
# Political Animals

# 9
# Choosing Your Battles

There are a number of popular aphorisms about timing, such as "Timing is everything," "There's a time and place for everything," and "To every thing there is a season, and a time to every purpose." Likewise, timing is critical for success when deciding which battles are worth fighting. You have to be aware of the political realities, including who has more power, workplace alliances, and the art of compromise and taking your time for the best opportunity. On some level, every workplace situation is like a "Survivor" show microcosm. You may not be isolated in a faraway place, stuck with minimal resources, but you still find the same kind of jostling for connections and position. And if you don't play the game well, you could be voted out of the office tribe.

I thought of these issues when a reader wrote me that he thought I was advising someone to "kiss ass," when I suggested the man should seek to avoid a conflict and work things out with someone who was a "troublemaker." The reader felt that one should have the "right to speak the truth" including exposing a very difficult person who played the victim and threatened legal charges.

But should one always do this? Sometimes yes and sometimes no. As they say in law school: "It depends."

Consider Sam's situation. He worked in an office where his boss, Darryl, had brought in Hal, the son of a close friend, as a trainee to learn the ropes. From the beginning, Sam felt Hal was unqualified and repeatedly made mistakes, although Darryl seemed to want to give Hal the benefit of the doubt. So Darryl simply corrected Hal's errors, told him to try harder, and encouraged other employees to help Hal. In turn, some of the other employees did help out by not only lending support and advice but sometimes by even doing Hal's work. Meanwhile, Sam was angry because he felt his own good work was not being recognized sufficiently, now that Darryl was paying more attention to Hal. Sam was further angered that other employees were bailing out Hal, when Sam thought Hal should be terminated. So should he speak up now? Hold his peace now or maybe forever? Or what?

# What Should Sam Do?

Here are some possibilities. In Sam's place, what would you do and why? And what do you think the outcomes of these different options would be?

 Point out what Darryl was doing wrong in the beginning, because nepotism is unfair and the other employees are doing Hal's work.

 Let Hal make mistakes, so Darryl will have to see that Hal is unqualified and eventually fire him. It's Darryl's problem; let him deal with it.

 Talk to Hal and tell him he isn't pulling his weight, and you and the other employees aren't willing to continue to cover for him.

 Talk to the other employees who are doing Hal's work and gain their support for a showdown to tell Hal he's got to do his work, because no one is going to continue doing it for him.

 Organize the other employees to complain to the boss about Hal as a group.

Other?

Eventually, what Sam decided to do is this. As much as he wanted to blow the whistle on Hal, he didn't, because he recognized the political landscape. He wasn't in a position of power in the office, and for now, Hal had the support of the head of the company, Darryl, and because of that the support of other employees. Thus, even though Hal wasn't doing a very good job, his work was getting done and the office was functioning smoothly. Under the circumstances, it wasn't politically wise for Sam to go into battle against Hal just now by speaking up and saying what he was really feeling. It was smarter for him to watch and wait, just as a good military commander does in deciding whether to advance now or whether there's too much risk of encountering an ambush.

But after a few months, when Hal continued to mess up and Sam sensed that Hal was no longer as protected by Darryl or other employees, he finally shared his opinions at a meeting about how to make the office more productive. Now his opinions were well accepted. As a result, over the next few weeks, Darryl put Sam in charge of the new office reorganization, and after a time, Hal left of his own accord, feeling he wanted to work in another type of company, so the problem worked itself out. In the process, Sam gained the appreciation of others in the office for speaking out when he did, and he felt a great surge of esteem on hearing their words of praise.

Thus, in the long run, Sam benefited by simply watching and waiting until the time was right, rather than speaking up too soon and potentially getting wounded himself. In a sense, he won the battle by not having to fight it—a kind of peace through strength and silence strategy, where you choose to strike when the timing is right, but remain silent and ready until then.

So, yes, to respond to my reader's comment, there are certainly times to speak the truth. But when—and if—you should do this depends on the circumstances, including your power position in the office, your support in an alliance, and how important it is to fight this particular battle. There are times when speaking the truth can be a good idea, such as when you have gathered evidence to show wrong-doing by another employee or supervisor, and you are psychologically prepared to take on the hostile territory that comes from being a whistleblower, including being forced out of your job.

But there are many other times when it is best to accept the political realities of a situation and not fight a particular battle, such as when you need to keep your job or when you need some time to gather evidence or personal support to back you up, rather than speaking up too soon and getting canned. Likewise, there are times when it may be better to smooth things over with a difficult person in the workplace, because he or she has support from others, is doing critically needed work, or could become your worst enemy, out for revenge and sabotage. In such cases, the dangers of speaking up outweigh the benefits of trying to smooth things over and seek an improved relationship. It may appear like "kissing ass" to those unfamiliar with the situation, but in fact, hesitating to speak up may be playing smart politics, until you find the right time, place, and strategy to strike back.

# Today's Take-Aways:

 Besides choosing your battles, choose the right time for them.

 Sometimes the best way to fight and win a battle is not to fight at all.

 Every workplace environment is political; so before entering a workplace battle, consider who has the power and whether you have the power to win.

# 10 Watch Out *for* Confidences

**B**ecoming someone's confidant at work can be flattering. You feel trusted with someone's secrets. You feel plugged in and are privy to behind-the-scenes gossip. You may experience a sense of power. You are consoling someone and giving advice, so you feel helpful and in the know. But if you are not wary, you can fall into the hidden pitfalls of being a confidant. What you know and what you share with a person who confides in you can backfire and blow up in your face.

That's what happened to Barbara, who became friendly with a co-worker, Nancy, in a sales and marketing department. They shared many things in common that drew them together: both were 30somethings from Boston, and both were interested in the local art scene. They got in the habit of having lunch together and occasionally called each other to discuss projects they were working on.

After a few weeks, Nancy began sharing more personal observations and concerns with Barbara. Nancy told Barbara how she was having a dispute with her landlord over a noisy tenant, and the landlord wasn't doing anything to fix the problem. Did Barbara think she should withhold some rent as an incentive, Nancy wondered, or did Barbara have other suggestions? Another time, Nancy described having problems with a designer who created a brochure for her. She complained the designer hadn't properly done the work and had claimed too many hours, so Nancy refused to pay her. Now the designer was threatening to sue. What did Barbara think she should do in response?

Barbara felt touched when Nancy first began sharing with her like a trusted friend, and so Barbara shared a few of her own problems in return—a dispute with a car salesman who overcharged her and a misunderstanding with a former employer about a commission that led her to quit the job. Several months later, as Nancy worked extra hours to increase her sales and move up the company ladder, Barbara felt privileged when Nancy began sharing her opinions about other salespeople at the company. Nancy did so at one lunch, when she described how different people in their department were performing or not performing up to expectations. Thereafter, Nancy continued to share such opinions, and a few times she complained to Barbara when people in other departments let her down, such as by giving her incorrect leads. In turn, Barbara shared her sympathy, support, or advice.

Barbara never questioned, however, whether listening to such information was appropriate. She never considered the dangers of sharing about herself. Instead, she felt honored that Nancy would confide in her, particularly since Nancy seemed on a fast track to move ahead.

But then it happened. One day Barbara and Nancy had their own dispute about who should get a particular lead, and Nancy accused Barbara of poaching on her territory. As the argument escalated, Nancy brought up Barbara's car dispute, commission misunderstanding, and some other problems Barbara had shared with her. "You have a lot of communication problems with people, don't you?" Nancy charged, and Barbara felt suddenly on the defensive, as Nancy used her previous confidences against her. Barbara also realized that Nancy's confidences over the year had pointed to a trail of problems with people. Barbara hadn't noticed the pattern before, because of her desire to help and her feelings of satisfaction at being the trusted friend.

But now Barbara suddenly found herself on the opposite side of the fence; Nancy now viewed her as one of the people who didn't perform properly. Though they continued to work in the same office, the lunchtime sharings and after-work phone chats came to an end. Instead, Barbara noticed that Nancy seemed to have an alliance with a recently hired employee. They went to lunch together, and Barbara imagined they had the same kind of conversations she once had with Nancy. Worse, Barbara worried that Nancy talked about her, and she was nervous what might happen if Nancy did well on the fast track and got promoted. Maybe someday Nancy could even be her boss.

# What Should Barbara Do?

Here are some possibilities. In Barbara's place, what would you do and why? What do you think the outcomes of these different options would be?

 From the start, before the problem with Nancy develops, ask her not to continue to share confidences, because you feel you need to keep personal relationships out of the workplace.

 Now that problems have developed, have a heart-to-heart conversation with Nancy to air out past grievances and make peace.

 Get friendly with the recently hired employee, so Nancy can't turn that employee against you.

 Notice when Nancy messes up at work, so you can quietly tip off the boss or others to keep her from being promoted.

 Let Nancy know that if she uses any of your confidences against you, you know plenty about her you can share, to keep her from using what you told her to harm you.

 Other?

You can find yourself in a dangerous situation when someone at work starts to share personal confidences with you—and when you share your own confidences in return. It can be tempting and flattering to be let into someone else's secrets. You can enjoy hearing the latest office gossip. You can gain a sense of power, privilege, and one-ups-manship when you hear someone dis others to you, since the person telling you seems to regard you more highly; otherwise, why would he or she confide these opinions of others' poor performance?

But the danger is **you** could be next. You could go from trusted confidant to being the subject of a confidence to someone else, as happened to Barbara. This is a risk that is especially great when someone shares confidences about their problems with other people. They have a pattern of problems—a trail of conflicts with others. And if you walk on that trail with them for too long, you can easily be left behind on it.

What if you have already trusted your confidences to someone else, have had a conflict, and fear your confidences are in danger of slipping out? At this point the cat could easily get out of the bag and you want to keep it in there. So what to do? Probably the best strategy at this point is the "let's work it out" conversation in which you diplomatically try to patch up past misunderstandings and suggest that you both honor what you have each told each other in confidence. Don't turn this conversation into one in which you threaten to tell if the other party does. A tit-for-tat exchange can easily escalate into an even greater cycle of revenge and backstabbing. Rather, use the art of diplomacy to appeal to the other person's best instincts. You can always think of ways to strike back with a counterattack later if your "let's be nice" strategy doesn't work. But for now, just keep it sweet and gentle to work on smoothing things over, so hopefully you don't have to get rough and tough later.

# Today's Take-Aways:

 If someone leaves a trail of conflicts with other people behind him or her, don't walk on the trail with that person. You're likely to get stuck on that trail yourself.

 Beware of the person who wants to fill you up with lots of confidences. A too-full glass can break, and you can be shattered like a broken glass yourself.

 If you do share confidences you later regret, play nice and seek an agreement to hold any confidences in secret; that way, if you can make peace now, you may not have to play rough and make war with someone who violates your confidences.

# 11
# When You're Not *in the* Family

Not being part of a family in a family-run business can make it more difficult for you—especially in smaller companies with several family members. In bigger companies, the influence of family members will generally be much diluted by the larger workforce and management team. Also, in a corporation, a commitment to shareholders and public record-keeping and reporting requirements will usually provide pressure to make sure family members are qualified and competent in their positions.

But what happens when you work with a group of family members who have more power than you in a smaller company, and you aren't part of the family? What can you do apart from leaving the company and finding another job? That's what one reader—let's call him Paul—wanted to know in asking for my views on nepotism.

Paul explained that he worked as a collection agent in a small collection agency with a dozen employees, where his immediate supervisor, David, and the head of operations, John, were brothers, and the president of the company, Frank, was their uncle. Before David got his job as supervisor, his father held the position until he retired a year earlier, and that's why David got the job after he graduated from college as a business major several years earlier. However, while Paul felt David did a good job and was very much qualified, he felt John, who also joined the company after college two years earlier did not do a good job and was not well qualified for his position. Though John's job was making sure the computer software, payroll system, and everyday administrative procedures worked effectively, foul-ups were frequent. Yet, whenever they happened, David commonly came to his brother John's defense, after which John worked on fixing the problem he had created by his errors.

Besides Paul, many other agents complained about John's work to each other, but they were afraid to say anything to David, because of his close relationship with his brother and others in the family, who handled various administrative tasks, such as payroll and advertising to get clients. While the agents, who worked on a draw and commission were not family members, the others who formed the power center of the company were. They felt David might even fire them to keep them quiet if they complained—or perhaps reduce their earnings by giving them harder leads for collection cases, given their commission against a draw arrangement. Paul thought the whole system was quite unfair.

# What Should Paul Do?

Here are some possibilities. In Paul's place, what would you do and why? What do you think the outcomes of these different options would be?

 Seek to become closer to David, the brother-supervisor, so you will become like one of the family, like David.

 Seek to do even more to help John, so John will realize how much he needs your help, which can lead to more advancement as John moves ahead.

 Talk to David, the supervisor, about the problem and seek to work out a solution that will result in positive changes for everyone.

Keep a chronology of what John is doing wrong to use in a discussion with David, the supervisor, or outside legal help.

 Talk to John and offer to help him improve his own performance.

 Other?

What should Paul do? Unfortunately, the system is unfair. But if you work in a small privately held company as a lower level or front-line employee, you may not be able to do much to make the overall system more just, unless the poorly performing family-member employee messes up so badly that he or she becomes a clear embarrassment and detriment to the company. Then, the family members are likely to move that person to a less vital position or even out of the company to reduce the threat. But barring such a clear-cut disaster, the incompetent family member will often continue to bumble along, perhaps protected by one or more other family members who cover for him, help him do the job, and clean up occasional mistakes. They may see this as helping out a weaker or disabled family member. This way, they get the work done, even though not in the most effective or efficient way, and non-family members may feel this is not a fair arrangement. Thus, if you are not in the family, adjusting to that situation may come with the territory of working in this particular company, even if you think this is not the best or fairest way to do the work.

One approach that might at least help you feel better about the situation is to try to understand the reasons other family members are sticking up for someone like John and learn to better accept this. This way you feel more comfortable working there, even if the situation seems unfair.

Alternatively, if this unqualified person is seriously hampering operations and upsetting many people by a lack of ability, maybe Paul— or anyone facing such a problem—could engage in various strategies to lead to change without losing a job for speaking up. The best option will depend on the particular circumstances and personalities involved.

For example, Paul might have a private meeting with David, his supervisor, to make him more aware of the extent of the problem and high level of dissatisfaction among other employees. He might also offer some suggestions for resolving the problem diplomatically, such as by providing John with additional training to do a better job. This greater awareness might help to produce positive changes, since David might view his role as occasionally coming to bat for his brother and may not recognize how serious the problem is. Once he does, he might then make effective changes. Thus, to promote awareness, Paul might start a chronology in which he keeps track of when John does something wrong that results in inefficiencies or losses to the company. Also, since there is strength and safety in numbers, Paul might get others who agree there is a problem to keep track as well.

Then, with the problem documented, Paul is in a better position to discuss the problem with his supervisor. He might also find it persuasive to approach the supervisor with one of his co-workers who is similarly upset by John's behavior. This way, once David sees how widespread the feelings against John are, he will likely take them more seriously—and then his commitment to the company and his staffers may well out-trump his commitment to protect his less competent brother.

Finally, another approach might be to consider why John is acting incompetently and what you or others might do to do to improve his performance. For example, maybe Paul has information to help John do a better job. Or maybe Paul could give John feedback on the weaknesses in the system he has set up (such as the difficulty of tracking a debtor's collections history), so John could figure out how to improve the system. In turn, providing this assistance might help to ingratiate Paul not only with John but also with others in the family, thereby improving his ability to move ahead or earn more money, despite a commission-based payment arrangement in a family-run firm.

In short, if you are faced with an unqualified family member in a family-run workplace, want to stay there, and can't overcome that family wall of protection, think of how you might help and join them. Be solutions-oriented and find ways to be supportive. The result might be that you not only solve the problem, but also help yourself get ahead, despite the bias toward hiring and promoting family members in the firm.

# Today's Take-Aways:

 Even if life and work are unfair, think how best to play the hand you've got.

 Don't just gripe about a problem as a group; by joining together, maybe you can solve the problem as a group.

 If you can help a family member in trouble, maybe the family will help you, too.

 Think of how you can contribute to the solution, by being solutions oriented. If you're not part of the solution, you're part of the problem, as they say.

# 12

## Dealing *with* Unearned Praise

E veryone likes getting praise, right? Everyone feels good when they are complimented, yes? Isn't that what thousands of managers want to learn to motivate people better and achieve increased productivity, correct?

Well, not always. Sure, most of the times these principles apply. But sometimes, if you feel you are getting unearned praised, you might not feel satisfied and motivated. In fact, you might feel unworthy, even suspicious about why someone is praising you for something you think you don't deserve. You might wonder if they have a hidden agenda.

Those kinds of issues came up when one woman, we'll call her Tanya, wrote to me asking: "What would you call receiving praise for something that you yourself thought to be just an ordinary, routine job, but someone else said was an exemplary performance?" She wrote to me because a woman she worked with on a project had praised her enthusiastically for some work she had turned in, but Tanya considered the work not to be very good, and she wasn't sure how to respond.

# What Should Tanya Do?

Here are some possibilities. In Tanya's place, what would you do and why? And what do you think the outcomes of these different options would be?

 Enjoy the praise. Even if you think you didn't deserve it, someone else does.

 Think about how the other person praised you, to decide if he or she really meant it, were just trying to be nice, or had other motives, and if so what. Then act based on what you think, though check out your suspicions before you act.

 Ask the person praising you to be more specific about what the praise is for to know better if he or she means it or is just saying it.

 If you think someone else really deserves the praise, tell the person praising you about what the other person has done; you can never go wrong honestly praising someone else.

 Don't take any praise too seriously. Treat it as just another everyday conversation, and keep doing what you do well, so you're doing a good job whether praised or not.

 Consider what to do better in the future, if you really think you did a lousy job, but the other person didn't realize this or is just praising you for other reasons.

 Other?

So what should she do? What should you do in a similar situation? As I replied to Tanya, I thought the first step was to assess her own perception of the activity and the other person's comment with a reality check. This way Tanya would have some basis for assessing her own perception and the other person's reaction in a more grounded, realistic way.

How do you get such a reality check? One way might be to review the requirements and expectations for the job. Another might be to get feedback from an independent party, perhaps even an expert in the field, to get an informed opinion of the quality of the work that was done. From this review, you might better understand the true merits of what you did.

You might even find out you did a better job than you realize. If so, consider whether you aren't giving yourself the proper credit for a good performance. Or perhaps you are holding too high expectations for yourself, so you think something isn't very good, when it really is. In this case, the praise is justified, and your perception of your performance is incorrect. Alternatively, if you really didn't do a good job and the other person is praising you to be supportive, for other reasons, or really didn't notice your poor work, consider how to do a better job in the future. Then, you'll really earn and deserve the praise you receive.

Another way to look at the issue of possibly unearned praise is to see whether you and the other person have different expectations or definitions of the performance and the outcome. For instance, if you think you should be doing an in-depth six-page analysis, you feel your brief interpretation is very superficial, while the other person only wants a two-page overview, and so thinks your longer assessment is really very good. In such a case, you both may be correct in your assessment, based on what you each thought the job was supposed to be. But you both have a communication problem, leading you to think you haven't lived up to expectations, while the other person thinks you have.

Alternatively, if you know you really have done a terrible job, and you believe that the other person probably knows this, you are dealing with insincere praise, which raises other questions about why it's given. For instance, the other person might be falsely praising you to keep you motivated or make you feel good. Or it may be the other person just wants to be liked by you out of a need for belonging or desire for friendship. In still other cases, you could be dealing with a hidden agenda, where someone is trying to flatter you falsely to get you to do something you don't want to do for them. Or maybe the person is so used to giving out praise whenever something is completed that he isn't sufficiently critical of the results.

Whatever the reason for this praise you don't think you deserve, it's important to figure out where it came from to help guide how you react. As an example, say the other person just wants to make you feel good or wants to be liked by you—then, no big deal. Perhaps just view the praise as an act of support or friendship, even if it's not merited; then acknowledge it and move on. By contrast, if you see this as insincere flattery by someone trying to manipulate you to do something you feel uncomfortable doing, then recognize the insincerity as a warning wake-up sign, and perhaps try to reduce your time working or interacting with that person. (Apart from thinking about how to deal with the person who has given you this questionable praise, consider what to do to improve so you will truly merit the praise you receive in the future.)

In short, there could be many different meanings of what has happened depending on the circumstances and the people involved. Start with a reality check to figure out the true quality of what you did. Then consider what this unearned praise really means to help you decide how to react in that situation. Look at how to do a better job if you really didn't perform up to par, regardless of how the other person intended the praise.

## Today's Take-Aways:

 Not sure whether you deserve the praise or not? Try a reality check to find out.

 Is someone giving you unearned praise? Maybe a hidden cost comes with it.

 If you're really sure the praise is unearned, ask if the other person knows this, and if so, why?

 Consider any unearned praise like a warning sign announcing that it's time to improve in the future, so you'll truly earn the praise you get.

# 13
# *T*he Blame Game

When things go wrong, it's a natural inclination to want to find out what went wrong and hope that someone or something else can be found at fault. After all, you don't want to take the blame and the consequences if you don't have to. And those with more power (i.e., managers) often look for those with less power (i.e., employees) to take the fall when problems occur. Everyone is essentially hoping to pass the buck in the blame game—and whoever ends up with the buck is out of the game or has to pay the penalty to stay in.

But sometimes the person passing the buck doesn't know. He or she doesn't recognize being responsible for creating a no-win situation that is doomed to fail. You might call this the "duck the blame by closing your eyes game." In effect, the whole game is poorly designed and doesn't play well—but no one wants to admit that he or she created a flawed design. What do you do if caught in such a "You're to blame!" situation, when someone with more power puts the blame on you? And what if he doesn't realize he is the one to blame, when he has more power to blame others?

That's what happened to Dave, a market research employee who had recently graduated with an M.A. in Organizational Development, when his company sent him to a training program to learn new research techniques for finding out more about how the company was doing. Dave was very enthusiastic, seeing this as an opportunity to advance to the next level as Project Manager. He arrived at the training, put on with the aid of an outside consulting team, with notebook in hand, eager to go.

"The goal is to get employees and managers talking about how they feel about the company, so you can look for what works well and where there might be problems," Sam, the outside consultant began, as Dave wrote down his comments. "You want not only to listen to what they say but observe how they are saying it. Then probe to learn more about their relationships with others in different departments."

"Of course, makes sense," Dave thought to himself, as Sam outlined the goals of the training. Dave also thought he could do a very good job, because he was an excellent interviewer, who had an easy rapport with others and was skilled at drawing people out. He had shown this on previous projects for the company and in his research at grad school.

But then, Sam began describing the process they would use. It wasn't straightforward interviewing. Instead, Dave wanted the researchers to use a diagram of a small town, so the interviewees could imagine they were in different roles in that town, from the mayor and members of the city council to small shopkeepers and visitors. The diagram even included a jail for placing criminals and an out-of-town motel by the airport where visitors could stay if passing through. Then, holding up a bag of crayons, Sam explained that the interviewees should use these to draw on the diagram. "You want the people you interview to place themselves and others in the company in the town. They should put all the major players there. Then, as they do, ask them to talk about what they are doing and ask them probing questions to get more in-depth information."

Sam passed out a script and list of sample questions to ask the interviewees as they drew. Plus, he explained, the researcher should tape and videotape the interviews and take some photographs for company records. "Oh, and you'll be doing these interviews with two employees and two managers at a time," Sam concluded. "That way you can get twice as many respondents in the same time to keep down costs for this project."

Then, the introductory explanation over, Sam used two assistants from his own training team to demonstrate how the interview and drawing process should work. For the next hour, he invited the trainees to ask questions, as his two assistants filled in their small towns with names of company departments and employees, drew in small symbols to express their feelings, and added in arrows to show different types of interactions. When they finished, their diagrams were awash with colors, lines, and scrawls of text, which Dave thought were confusing, and afterwards the session continued with more discussion about what they had put in their pictures and why.

Finally, after Sam invited the trainees: "Now try it yourself," Dave and the other trainees paired up to take turns interviewing each other using the diagram. But not only did Dave find it awkward trying to draw and transport his everyday experience to the diagram, but he found it hard to create symbols to express his ideas. When he led the interview himself, he found it hard to frame the questions, as he thought about all he had to do to guide his partner through the drawing process. "So why not ask the questions you want to know directly?" Dave wondered. "Why create this imaginary small town to evoke their answers in the first place?"

Then, in the follow-up debriefing session to discuss the experience, Dave had even more questions, since the process seemed to contradict everything he had learned about good interviewing, such as interviewing people one at a time to develop a close rapport and to get them to share with you in confidence. He additionally felt all the equipment created a barrier, too, since normally, when photographs or films were needed to document an activity or interview, a photographer came along to do that, so the researcher could concentrate on the research. Or if the researcher took his or her own photos, such as to make a presentation of research results, he came back later to take the photos, so as not to interfere with the process of interviewing and observing. But now he was expected to do it all at the same time—conduct the interview, photograph the interviewees, and record some of the interviews on videotape. In short, the whole research protocol that Sam was presenting didn't seem to make sense, though the director of the research department, Frank, had presented Sam as a highly regarded expert.

Thus, in the debriefing process, Dave raised some of questions about the research process. "Why are we doing two interviews at a time? How did you happen to develop the small town model? Why can't we take the photos after the interview or have someone else come in to take them?" Some of the reasons Sam gave were: because of budget considerations, to get at deeper information, or to make the interview process fun, though Dave still remained quietly skeptical. Even so, he was determined to do the interviews as best he could. After all, this was his job.

But after the session broke up, Frank, the research department director, asked him to come into his office. Somberly, he closed the door, sat down behind his desk, looked straight at Dave, and told him: "Look, I'm sorry but you're off the employee interview project." Dave was dumbfounded and nearly speechless. "But why what's wrong?" he stammered.

"Because this project just doesn't seem to be a good fit for you."

"But why? How? Is it because I asked too many questions?" Dave wondered.

"No, no," Frank tried to reassure him. "This project just calls for quite a bit of flexibility and being part of a team." With that, Frank opened the door, so Dave could leave and return to his usual research work.

As he left, Dave felt disappointed and crushed that Frank wasn't even willing to consider his questions about any problems with the research design and instead blamed him for not being a good fit. Plus now, given what happened, he felt he would be out of the running for any chances for a promotion to a project manager. He had felt so sure there was something wrong with the proposed interview process, but now he questioned his own abilities and wondered about his future with this company. So what should he do?

# What Should Dave Have Done and What Should He Do Now?

Here are some possibilities. In Dave's place, what would you have done or do and why? What do you think the outcomes of these different options would be?

Get with the program no matter what you think of it. Questioning your boss or the experts isn't the way to get ahead.

 Stay silent at the training, but raise your concerns with your boss afterwards. This way he may be more likely to listen, since he isn't worried about saving face in front of the group because of doubts expressed at the training itself.

 Raise your concerns about the project, and if they aren't addressed and you're blamed for raising these issues, leave the company.

 Just listen and observe at the training, and be ready to troubleshoot and propose another research design when problems arise, to show off your skills.

 Tell Frank's boss that the research program isn't working, and be ready to take the consequences for going over Frank's head if his boss doesn't listen. It may become more difficult to work with Frank if you stay, and you may find yourself out of a job.

 Other?

Unfortunately, Dave's story illustrates what happens when a myopic management is committed to a particular approach and doesn't want to hear any input that something could be wrong with their planned initiative. Here it was a research program, but it could be any kind of plan. The problem is that instead of welcoming possible criticisms in the early stages to make changes and avoid problems down the road, Frank was already committed to the program. So he had on his blinders by placing his confidence in the know-how of an outside expert. Instead, he would have gotten better insight had he sought input to assess for himself how the new research plan might work and be prepared to make any needed changes and improvements.

In a sense, Dave's difficulties with the research protocol and his questions pointed to problems with that research design, though Frank didn't see it and instead blamed Dave for not being a good team player who would participate in the project. Most likely, his quick decision to place the blame on Dave was his way of shutting out any consideration that the plan might be wrong; this way he could stick to the plan without having to face any further concerns about it from Dave.

So what about Dave? And what should anyone do in a similar situation where those in power appear to be committed to a program that seems to be flawed in design? Unfortunately, those with the most knowledge don't always have the most power to implement that knowledge, though ideally a more enlightened management would encourage those in the know to come forward. They would welcome and invite such questions, see any objections and concerns as an early warning sign of problems ahead, and make the changes.

But if they don't, the question becomes what to do if you are faced with a myopic management. Do you play the office politics game and remain quiet to get ahead? Or do you ask questions and reveal your reservations like Dave did? There is no one answer, since it depends on your personal values and practical considerations, such as whether you can find another job in a tight market.

If you have to go along to get along, it may be wise to do the best you can to participate in a project, even if the design is flawed, and go with the flow as problems arise, so that the project has to be either changed or canned. Sometimes it makes the most sense for you to play the game, even if the game itself is poorly designed, if you want to get ahead and avoid getting blamed for something that's not your fault, such as when good jobs are few and far between.

On the other hand, if you can, it may be much better to find another game to play with another, better designer, which is what Dave eventually did. After thinking about what happened, he realized he needed to trust what he already knew about good research and interviewing design, not rely on what he perceived as an error by his boss and outside expert. Rather than taking the undeserved blame which dimmed his prospects in a company with a manager who blamed him rather than the new program, he decided it was time to leave. Despite the tight job market, he had saved up enough to take a year to look for a job and try doing some freelance research assignments. He left the company, leaving the blame game behind to find another game where he had a better chance to win. Meanwhile, over the next few weeks the research project ran into the kinds of problems that Dave had raised questions about, leaving Frank to find someone else to blame if he could, rather than taking the blame himself.

# Today's Take-Aways:

 Before you take the blame in the blame game, consider whether you really deserve it. Maybe it belongs to someone else.

 Just because you don't have the position or the power doesn't mean you aren't right.

 If someone has trouble getting with a new program, it may mean the problem is with the program—not with the person.

 Before you place blame on someone for doing something wrong, consider why he or she is doing it wrong. Maybe there's something wrong with the way you are giving instructions or with the instructions themselves.

 If you raise your objections, but no one listens, rather than expecting a raise where you are, think about how to raise yourself up and out to somewhere else. But take your time to make the climb to another mountain—there's no need to try to climb too quickly, or you may fall off.

# 14

# Besting
## *the* Betrayer

What do you do when someone you have trusted with information turns around and uses that information to advance his or her own career? Worse, what if that person tries to go into competition with you? The problem can occur whether you hire someone, work with a partner, or team up with someone in your own company. You provide the ideas and leadership; then someone co-opts your ideas or takes the credit. Unless you want to let that person get away with it, you've got to do something. But what?

That was Bill's dilemma when he teamed up with a partner from another company. His own small product development company needed some help in turning a design into a new product, and Bill was assigned to find an outside design company to help develop the idea and make the prototype on a partnership basis. Bill's boss Ralph felt the company was too busy with current orders and production to do the additional design work, and Bill thought he knew the perfect person to do this—Jerry, who had previously worked in his department, but had recently started his own small design company. Who better to work with on the highly secret product design than a former co-worker who had become a friend? Bill and Jerry still talked on the phone every few weeks and went out for an occasional drink to catch up on old times.

When Bill contacted Jerry he expressed great enthusiasm for creating the prototype. "Sure, I'm your man," he said, explaining that he could jump right on the project and give it priority attention, since it had been slow getting his new company off the ground. He also talked about how he could help Bill's company sell and promote the idea once the prototype was ready, pointing out that he had been putting together his own Web site and database to promote his own company.

So Bill thought the arrangement was ideal, and a few days later he dropped off the plans for the prototype. He also gave Jerry a short partnership letter that described how their two companies would split any proceeds 50–50 after deducting costs.

Thus, everything seemed fine when Bill reported the arrangement to his boss, Ralph, who also thought it was a good choice. "A great way to help out a former employee," Ralph commented. "Keep it all in the family."

At first everything seemed to go smoothly. Jerry gave Bill reports of how things were going every few days, describing how he was using the illustrations and blueprints Bill gave him to make preliminary and then final models. But after a few weeks Jerry called to say he was unexpectedly ill and had to go into the hospital for tests.

Bill tried to be understanding, especially since Jerry was an old friend and had already spent several weeks on the project. Besides, Bill told his boss Ralph, "We're so far along. It'll only be a few more weeks." So they waited, holding off their own planned introduction of the product, while Jerry recovered at home and gradually resumed working on the project.

Or was that actually what happened? Bill suddenly began to wonder himself, when one day he was doing some research on the Internet, recalled how Jerry had mentioned he was designing a Web site to promote his new company, and decided to check it out. And there on one of Jerry's Web pages was an announcement of a great new product line he was introducing—with photographs that looked very much like the product design illustrations he had originally brought to Jerry. When Bill called Jerry, Jerry seemed flustered as he first stammered and stumbled, but then quickly recovered and offered an explanation: "Oh, I was just going to help promote our project, since I said I could help promote it. So I thought I'd test out some photos on my site."

But was that really the case? Bill hung up feeling like he had caught a kid with his hands in the cookie jar. He wasn't even sure if Jerry had really been ill or just buying time to run with the idea himself, and he wasn't sure what to do now.

# What Should Bill Do?

Here are some possibilities. In Bill's place, what would you do and why? What do you think the outcomes of these different options would be?

 Accept Jerry's explanation and figure he was just flustered, because he was surprised before he was ready to tell you about his Web site.

 Talk to Ralph and tell him what happened, so he can deal with Jerry.

 Call Jerry to say that you don't believe his explanation that he was just trying to promote the design as partners, and tell him the partnership is over.

 Arrange a meeting with Jerry to share your suspicions that Jerry was trying to promote the model as his own and maybe wasn't even sick, and give Jerry the benefit of the doubt.

 Call a lawyer to send Jerry a cease and desist order and formally dissolve any partnership.

 Other?

Unfortunately, betrayals can be tricky when you think you have been shafted by someone, but aren't really sure. When the possible betrayal involves a co-worker or friend you have trusted for a long time, the situation is even worse. You can feel torn between wanting to give the person the benefit of the doubt and feeling even more betrayed, because this isn't just a working arrangement gone sour but a personal relationship on the rocks, too.

In this case, as I advised Bill, a first step is to separate your feelings of betrayal from what actually happened, and then, after considering reasonable possibilities, trust your gut. Also, Bill should consider that if Jerry tried to pursue the project on his own, maybe to kick-start his struggling company, and lied about doing this, he might lie again in any confrontation. So barring bringing in a PI to investigate what really happened, Bill might never know Jerry's true intentions in posting an announcement about the new product.

At the very least, Jerry is guilty of not telling Bill about his promotional ideas. But knowing the importance of keeping this project secret until ready to launch, why would Jerry not at least ask Bill if it was okay to post such an announcement? In short, even giving Jerry the benefit of the doubt, what he did is either the result of poor communication or bad judgment. It also seems likely that Jerry might have had a good economic reason to do what he did, even if it meant shafting a former co-worker and friend. After all, his company is struggling; Bill has just brought him plans and he is able to make the product; and there's only a short letter of understanding from Bill's company about partnership proceeds. It's reasonable that he could have thought he might run with the idea himself, and Bill's gut feeling of betrayal could very probably be right. But even if the betrayal cannot be proved, once you do have those strong feelings of betrayal, there's probably little hope of restoring trust. Bill would probably continue to question Jerry's intentions and loyalty, and so any partnership is very likely doomed.

Thus, Bill should focus on the best way of ending the relationship as smoothly as possible and doing what he can for damage control to prevent Jerry from capitalizing on the project. And that's what he did. He first went to Ralph to explain the situation, since Ralph had previously employed Jerry and had given his go-ahead on Jerry's involvement. Then, he set up a meeting to have a discussion with Jerry, giving him a chance to explain his side of what happened. Even though he didn't trust what Jerry was saying, the meeting was at least a way for Jerry to save face by claiming he had good intentions in setting up the Web site promotion.

Then, Bill explained that because of what happened, whatever Jerry's intentions in posting the page on the site, he didn't have the same good feelings about working with Jerry as a partner any longer. Nevertheless, he hoped to work out something to compensate Jerry for his time in making the model. And so without the need for expensive lawyers and in a spirit of "let's both make the best of a bad situation," a deal was struck. Bill paid Jerry a small amount, terminated the partnership, and got the model from him, along with a signed agreement that Jerry wouldn't try to sell a product with the same design. Bill knew he could always monitor Jerry's Web site to make sure he complied, which he did over the next few months.

The problem was resolved fairly quickly, and Bill felt comfortable that the main loss was his feeling of trust in Jerry, along with what he had once considered a continuing friendship with a former co-worker. Even though Jerry later sent him some photographs he had taken of the model with the note: "Just thought you might be able to use these" as a peace gesture, Bill didn't speak to Jerry again. But he did use the photos. Why not? He and his company had more than paid for them in the feelings of betrayal and loss of trust that lingered long after the incident was over. Later on, when others in the industry came to Bill or Ralph asking about Jerry's work, since they knew he had once worked at their company, they simply said they couldn't recommend him, without explaining why. Jerry never did get his struggling company off the ground. He had been betrayed by his own likely betrayal, even if Bill didn't know for sure, but just had an intuition about it.

Likewise, if you are in a similar situation where you feel someone you trusted has betrayed you, say by using work you have done without giving you credit or fair compensation, a good approach is to find ways to make the best of the situation. You may not have solid proof; the person may come up with innocent explanations. But if you still feel a strong sense that the person isn't being honest with you and is just coming up with cover up excuses, you could very well be right. Our intuition often works as a survival mechanism to give us feelings when something isn't right and it's best to get away.

Thus, if you believe strongly that a betrayal has occurred, it's best to operate on the principle that you can't trust this person again in the future. For once trust is gone, it's often gone for good. What takes weeks and years to build can quickly evaporate in a moment, like a sudden break in a strong bridge. You might have crossed it many times while it was standing; but once it quickly crumbles down, it takes years to repair.

Therefore, assuming trust is gone, try to end things as diplomatically and finally as possible, such as by negotiating some kind of end-it agreement, so you part on relatively good terms. There's no need to have to prove it or bring in the lawyers, except as a last resort. Rather, as Bill did, seek a comfortable way to disengage and then move on. You might, as one person once told me, put what's in the past in your rear-view mirror. Then, look forward and drive ahead.

# Today's Take-Aways:

 Once trust is gone, it's gone. It's very difficult to bring it back, and it's hard to want to try.

 When you feel someone has betrayed you, give him a chance to explain, though don't necessarily believe him. Consider the facts and what you feel in your gut.

 Betrayals are like broken bridges; but rather than blowing them up because they're broken, think of ways to repair them or defuse the damage. Then look for another bridge that's solid for an easier, surer crossing in the future.

 When a betrayer gets caught, he or she can be like the kid found with a hand in the cookie jar who says "I didn't do it" to get your approval and acceptance again. But while it's good to clean up the crumbs by being diplomatic, it's best not to provide the betrayer with another chance at the cookie jar; it's better to close it up tight and move on.

# PART III

# Ethical Dilemmas

# 15

# Don't Let Them "Ethics" You

Some people pride themselves on being "ethical," and being "ethical" is certainly a quality to strive for. Not only does acting ethically mean you show honorable character traits, like being honest, square-dealing, and following moral principles, but other people feel they can trust you and are more likely to be loyal, motivated, committed, and productive.

However, the problem comes when people define ethics very broadly to include any behavior they think is wrong, unjust, or unfair, so they can claim the moral ground in a situation that is not really an ethical issue. Rather, what they are objecting to as unethical behavior is simply another perfectly acceptable way of doing business—and even a common practice in certain industries. Thus, when one person accuses you of being "unethical," it may be simply because they have different definitions of what's fair or right than you do. In that case, don't let their accusations of unethical behavior guilt-trip you to do what they think you should do; instead, regard their accusation as simply their opinion or belief. Then, let the best strategy be your guide, rather than letting their definition of what's ethical or what isn't guide you. If the issue isn't an ethical dilemma, don't make it one or get drawn into a debate about ethics. Where differing opinions trigger charges of being unethical, the other person usually has strongly felt emotions, and when that's the case, it's hard to change anyone's mind.

Such an attempt to turn a difference of opinion into an accusation of being unethical is what happened to Devon when he was Allen's partner in a new business. They entered into an agreement with Tom to promote his new Web site designed to link people selling craft items to prospective buyers. Devon and Allen agreed to promote Tom's site actively in exchange for a one-third commission from sales they generated. Their promotion work would include sending out releases, creating a dedicated Web site, and providing direct links from their own site, which was devoted to promoting artists. In return, Tom agreed to pay a commission for each order.

After Devon set up the site and drafted a few releases, Tom thought they were great, and everything seemed fine, until Tom signed his first client, a very difficult artist, who needed a lot of advice on how to set up and price his items to sell them on line. Though Tom charged the artist for this help, he wrote to Devon saying he thought the originally agreed upon 35% commission on orders for sales was too high to pay on his hourly consulting work. So, Devon responded with a counter-offer, proposing just 10% on the consulting fees, since 10% referral fees were common in the industry. Tom now not only objected to paying any referral fee for his consulting, but also questioned the 35%, claiming it was too high for just a link, when he was paying others at most only 25%. Though Devon pointed out that he and Allan were doing more than providing a link since they had set up a dedicated site and were writing press releases, Tom was still not mollified.

Then, before Devon could explain or propose another counter-offer, his partner Allen chimed in, afraid they might lose the client entirely. But instead of recognizing this as a difference of opinion about fees and everyday business practices, Allen sought to turn the conflict into one with ethical dimensions. "Why are you going after his consulting fees?" he wrote in an urgent e-mail questioning Devon's request for a commission on Tom's fees. "Tom is just doing his job to get people to the site to sell the service. So that's not fair; so it's unethical to ask for a commission on that."

But while being too demanding might lose the sale, was it unfair and unethical? Devon didn't think so, since referral fees were a standard business practice in many industries and he especially resented Allan's "I'm right" attitude in framing the conflict with Tom in ethical terms. How could Allan dare to question his ethics, when this was just a simple matter of negotiating an agreement to get the best deal? He didn't think he was being unethical, just trying for the best deal he could, and he felt angry with Allan for questioning his ethics on an issue that didn't involve ethics at all. So what should Devon do?

# What Should Devon Do?

Here are some possibilities. In Devon's place, what would you do and why? What do you think the outcomes of these different options would be?

 Ignore Allan's claims that he is being unethical and wait for Tom to respond to his latest offer.

 Write a detailed memo to Tom explaining why the referral rate is fair, because Tom is getting extra work, and give a copy to Allan to show him this isn't an issue of ethics.

 End the arrangement with Tom, because he is trying to change the original agreement and can't be trusted, and explain this to Allan, his partner.

 Stop doing extra promotional work for Tom and accept a reduced commission rate, and tell Allan this is what you decided to do.

 Drop any claim for a referral fee, since Tom feels this isn't fair and Allan thinks the claim is unethical, even if you disagree and are just seeking a better bargain.

Other?

I nitially, Devon was inclined to be more persuasive to convince Tom and Allan that he was simply asking for an arrangement that is standard in many industries and be more convincing in explaining that there was nothing unfair or unethical about his proposed arrangement.

Yet after taking a night for further reflection, Devon decided that even though he thought he was being quite reasonable and his offer was not at all unfair or unethical, since the referral was giving Tom additional work, he decided to back down. One concern was that if Tom thought the referral fee was unfair and unethical, however unjust the accusation, he could easily respond by being unethical himself by doing the work without telling Devon and Allen. Another problem was creating more conflicts with his own partner should Tom do this or walk away from their original deal. Thus, as much as he saw the issue as just a simple fee dispute, not a question of ethics, he felt it was best strategically to back down. Besides, most referral fees wouldn't result in consulting fees anyway. That's what Devon did, dropping any claim for the additional commission, and dropping any further discussion about the question of ethics. Though he didn't think ethics had anything to do with the issue in the first place, he decided it was best to let Tom and Allen think their arguments about fairness and ethics had won out; that was the most practical thing to do.

Similarly, if you're placed in such a position, in which you don't think the issue is an ethical one but others do, look at it strategically. In some cases, it might be worth discussing to explain why there is no ethical consideration involved. But if that discussion is likely to inflame matters by turning a debate about business considerations into accusations about who is ethical and who isn't, then do what's most practical under the circumstances. You'll generally end up with a more peaceful work or business relationship that way.

# Today's Take-Aways:

 Don't get into a debate about who's ethical and who isn't if someone raises an ethical flag. You'll only spread more flames than light.

 As long as you think you are doing what's ethical, do what's practical when confronted by differing opinions about what's ethical and what's not.

 Sometimes the accusation of being unethical is more like a club to force you to do what someone else wants—not really a true guide to what's ethical in a situation where ethics isn't involved.

 When someone tries to "ethics" you, it's generally best not to fight back with "ethics" yourself—you'll only end up in an ethics match, and you both could lose.

# 16

# When Somebody Wants *to* Change *the* Rules

Certainly in today's fast-paced and changing business world, it makes sense to change the rules. You've got to adapt, and change, innovation, reengineering, transformation, and like words have a with-it cachet. Though people often resist saying goodbye to old habits, in time, most will change, and generally change is for the good, since it leads to better ways of doing things.

Yet sometimes, change does not work and backfires in the long run, such as when you change previously established rules to which everyone has agreed without getting their agreement. You may not know it at the time, because people may be afraid to state their feelings of resistance, but tensions and resentment can build up. Then, the change you want may lead to changes you don't, because the change breaks bonds of trust. You may not see the results right away—but down the road, watch out.

That's what happened when Brad entered into a partnership agreement with Perry to start a mail order business selling unique personalized premiums such as mugs, calendars, and banners. Brad and Perry had had great rides during the dot.com boom, but after a year of part-time and temporary jobs, both were struggling to make ends meet. But since Brad still had some credit left on his credit cards, he offered to provide the small amount of funds they needed to get started—about

$1000 for a name, stationery, business cards, and small classified ads. The understanding was that the first funds would go to pay Brad back and then they would share the proceeds 50–50. Sure, Perry agreed, and they started off using Brad's living room, kitchen, and garage to set up the shipping arrangements. While it was Brad's job to locate the products and suppliers and handle most of the customer contact to make the sale, Perry's job was getting the leads, organizing them, and sending out the orders. Meanwhile, they each continued to work at odd jobs and assignments as they could, spending about 20 hours each week on the business.

Unfortunately, it took a little longer than expected to get off the ground, because of the time needed to get all their sales materials together and organize their leads. Still Brad and Perry seemed to have a great working relationship, and Perry began to confide in Brad about his own difficulties in making it from day to day. "I used to be making great money," he said. "But not now." Meanwhile, Brad was having his own problems with nearly maxed out credit cards, though he didn't want to burden Perry with his situation, given Perry's dire straights. At least some money was starting to come in from the business, more and more each month, and Brad was able to start paying himself back. Brad estimated that in about a month they would both start sharing the proceeds, as he told Perry. "We're so close to break-even. Just a few more weeks."

Then everything exploded. Perry sent Brad a letter stating that he wanted at least $300 now because he was so broke, or he would stop working on the business entirely. As he explained, he had told some friends about how he couldn't make money from the business until the business broke even, but then his friends told him that arrangement was ridiculous. Instead, they stated firmly, even though incorrectly, that typically in partnerships the first thing the partners should do after making money from a sale was to pay the partner and then pay the bills. Besides, Perry claimed, a part-time job he was training for might develop into something more. So now he wanted his share of the income from the few recent sales they had had plus his share of each future transaction. Or if Brad wanted to end the partnership, Perry concluded: "You can pay me for the work I have done and I'll turn over the list of leads and other materials I put together for the business."

Brad was floored by the sudden request and wasn't sure what to do.

# What Should Brad Do?

Here are some possibilities. In Brad's place, what would you do and why? What do you think the outcomes of these different options would be?

 Refuse Perry's demand for more money and remind him that the original agreement was to pay you back first. Besides, Perry has too much stake in the business to simply bail out and is probably bluffing.

 Agree to send Perry a check to gain his continued cooperation, but then don't send the check, since he probably no longer expects it after his apology.

 Send Perry the check in the spirit of good will, accept Perry's apology, and continue with the partnership as if nothing happened, since Perry has made amends.

 Refuse to let Perry's threat browbeat you regardless of the consequences, and find another line of business without Perry.

 Other?

**B**arry's conundrum was that he felt he couldn't continue the business without the leads or Perry handling the orders. But he also felt like Perry was suddenly holding him up, changing their original agreement by fiat. So should he confront Perry directly? Placate him? Or what?

Finally, Brad did the one thing that seemed to resolve the situation for the moment. He wrote back to Perry, telling him that he would send him a check for $300, though he also complained that "I'm a partner, too." He pointed out that, in addition, he had advanced about $2000 toward the business, including his initial $1000 payment, using the first payments to pay himself back. Plus, he explained that with his own high credit card debts and house mortgage, his own financial situation was close to collapse. Finally, he emphasized how the key to the success of the business was to bring in more orders, so they both could get compensated—and they needed only about a dozen more at this point.

Fortunately, Brad's letter broke the log jam, since Perry responded that he hadn't taken into account some of the extra expenses Brad had incurred, because "I forgot about them." Perry apologized for coming on so strong that he appeared to threaten the continued survival of the business if Brad didn't pay up right way. "I only asked to be compensated for my time. I wasn't trying to undermine anything." In addition, he agreed to work even harder after he took a short break to finish up training for his part-time job, working on both if necessary.

Yet, for Brad, Perry's apology wasn't enough to put aside what had happened. The damage had already been done by Perry's request to change the rules, and it still wasn't clear if Perry's apology meant he no longer was asking for a payment, since he sent a separate message thanking Brad for saying he would send the check. Just in case, Brad did send Perry the $300. But he also began looking for another partner or a way to carry on the business on his own once he got the information he needed from Perry. So on one level it may have seemed like business as usual. But while trying to maintain an appearance of "everything's fine" Brad was preparing for a future without Perry.

Why the dual strategy and deception? Brad realized how dependent he was on Perry, so he felt he had to give him what he wanted to gain his cooperation, even if Perry had backed off from his demand. At the same time, his feelings of trust in his partner were gone, so in the future, he wanted to end that dependency link; he wanted to work with someone he could trust. Thus, while Perry might have gotten what he wanted in the short term, he had undermined the long-term relationship. Outwardly, everything might have appeared like the relationship returned to the way it was, but Perry's actions had led Brad to become devious in return. While he was acting like all was fine again, even sending the money because Perry needed it, Brad was looking toward the future— one without Perry, because Perry had threatened to change the rules.

Similarly, think carefully if you are in a situation where you would like to change an agreement. Be very careful what you ask for, because you might get it, only to find out that in the long term, you are not getting what you really want. Alternatively, if you're in a situation where someone suddenly changes the rules on you, consider what to do from both a short-term and a long-term perspective. As in Brad's case, an initial strategy might be to go along with the rule change, if the alternative is worse, such as undermining your business or work relationship entirely. But then, consider what else you might do in the future when the initial threat is gone—such as finding another partner you can trust or finding a way to do the work yourself (say by hiring an assistant), once the person you don't trust is out of the picture.

# Today's Take-Aways:

 Before you try to change the rules, think how someone else is going to feel about those changes. He or she needs to understand and agree to those rule changes, too.

 If you try to change the rules using threats about how valuable you are, you might be giving someone a good reason to find they can do without your value in the future.

 If someone tries to force a rule change on you, think about the best strategy. Maybe it would be worth agreeing to change the rules right now, but you can make your own rule changes later to make things right.

# 17

# When There's a Betrayer in the Group

W e read about leaks in government and business all the time. Someone expresses his or her disapproval by leaking a memo or embarrassing story, and most of the time the leaker isn't caught and it's not worth pursuing. While many of the big stories of secret information that leaks end up on the evening news, everyone has private thoughts or personal information they don't want shared with others at work. When that happens—when a leak is very up-close and personal— it can feel really devastating to the victim. It can also undermine trust and sharing within a group, because no one knows who the leaker is and whether he or she will leak again.

That's what happened when Sylvia joined an online support group for research and editorial employees who worked at different companies. The idea was to have a private network for employees who were doing a similar job at different companies around the country to share their experiences, both good and bad. They could even talk about their reactions to different managers and supervisors and give each other advice on how best to get ahead in the field. Everyone got a password, and out of about 400 interested employees around the United States, about 40–50 members became part of a regular core group, while another 100 or so network members checked in from time to time with questions or opinions.

《 93 》

For awhile, everything seemed fine, and many employees viewed this as even more than a group for sharing work experiences and tips. They came to see many members of the group as friends, even if they didn't meet personally, much like they did others in the field they met in their own location. Then one of the participants, Joyce, commented on how Teresa, one of several supervisors who gave her assignments, had been unreasonable and unsympathetic. Though Joyce once had a great relationship with Teresa, she felt Teresa was now very insistent about her meeting a deadline sooner than was necessary, meaning that Joyce would have to work over a weekend and give up an event she was hoping to attend. Why? Joyce surmised it was because Teresa was herself under pressure and so wanted the project extra early to be sure she got it on time and give it an extra review. "But she doesn't need it," Joyce complained. "I've always turned in my work on time and complete, so she doesn't need to do any extra work. Why now?"

The group in turn was very sympathetic with suggestions on what to do, from looking for help on the project to research resources to make it go more quickly, so maybe Joyce could take her trip after all. Thus, Joyce went to work the following day thinking the matter was all resolved only to find that Teresa was furious. Apparently, Teresa had heard about Joyce's online complaint and was angry about what Joyce had said about her—though she wouldn't say how she found out. Potentially, it might have been someone who also worked in the company, though it could have been someone who met Teresa at a networking meeting or even someone who knew someone Teresa knew who passed on the information to Teresa. Whatever the source of the news, the upshot was that Teresa pulled the project from Joyce, told Joyce to take a few days unpaid vacation time, and wouldn't tell her who had told her what Joyce allegedly said. Now, not only was her private communication rendered public, but Joyce felt her relationship with Teresa was irretrievably damaged, too.

Besides being disturbed by the encounter with Teresa, Joyce was devastated by what she felt was a betrayal by a group member. Who was it, and what did others in the group think about what happened? That night Joyce sent an e-mail message describing what happened, and within hours, the response was electric. Others in the group not only sympathized with her but were outraged by what happened. They described the leaker as a "mole," a "Judas," a "spy," and many called for that person to come forward and apologize or for the group as a whole to sniff out the leaker. Then, e-mails went back and forth speculating about who the leaker might be and complaining about how they, too, felt betrayed by someone who undermined what they thought was a private, confidential place. They would no longer feel safe to share their thoughts freely.

Meanwhile, while this sharing of hurt, angry feelings went on, others posted suggestions on different ways to smoke out the culprit—from going to Teresa and demanding she reveal the leaker to analyzing who was most likely to know and tell Teresa. Sylvia even proposed her theory that the leaker might be jealous of Joyce's close relationship with Teresa or feared that Joyce might be promoted for her good work, thus depriving the leaker of a desired spot by a promotion or a transfer into the company. Still another woman suggested finding the leaker by looking at those who didn't post their outrage, whereupon another participant said: "No, that's not the way, since the leaker could well be among us and could be using this outrage to conceal the truth."

In short, the online debate turned very ugly because most of the participants felt deeply betrayed by what had happened, and some even felt more upset than Sylvia, because this place that had been so important to them no longer felt secure and safe. Though one group member suggested that this leak to Teresa might have been an inadvertent slip of the tongue or maybe the leaker mentioned what Joyce said to a friend who told Teresa or someone else did, no one cared about exactly how the information had gotten to Teresa. Regardless of what happened, the group's privacy had been violated, and many worried that the group might never feel safe again. If the leaker were online, it was unlikely that he or she would dare to come forward, since the group's anger was so great. The group was at a kind of crossroads, as Joyce, Sylvia, and many other core members debated what to do in response to the leak.

# What Should Joyce Do?

Here are some possibilities. In Joyce's place, what would you do and why? What do you think the outcomes of these different options would be?

 Drop out of the group. Not only is it no longer secure because of the betrayal, but there has been too much anger for it to become supportive again.

 Invite the leaker to come forward, if not to the group as a whole, then to you personally, since you now want to forgive and let go.

 Explain to Teresa that you were only sharing some general opinions in a private group, and the report about your comments was misunderstood and told to her out of context. Then try to patch up the relationship from there.

Stay in the group, but be more careful about what you share in the future. Should you want to disclose personal or negative information, share it with a few selected others privately, but not with the whole group.

Other?

W as there anything the group could do at this point? Or was the value of the support group irretrievably lost? I only heard about what happened several weeks after the incident, and gradually the fury about it did die down. Most people felt that since Teresa wasn't talking and the leaker wasn't coming forward to admit any guilt, they would probably never be able to identify the leaker in their midst. There was not much to do about it, and the group turned to sharing information on other issues. Still, the betrayal had long, deep roots that people remembered, such as when occasionally someone held back and was more cautious in what she said. She felt reluctant to talk about anything very personal, since she was afraid it might go beyond the group.

Unfortunately, in a situation where the betrayer could be almost anyone and the likelihood of finding out who it is is low, there might be little you or anyone else can do to resolve the situation. But you could still work out arrangements for the future to help group members feel more protected and thereby preserve the group, which is what some group members did. For example, the group members now continue to share openly about nonsensitive matters, and when someone wants advice or support for a personal issue, they can invite people to respond privately off the list. Another possibility for protecting privacy is setting up a smaller subgroup to share on personal issues, and posting or distributing by e-mail the names of all members of the subgroup. so everyone knows who is participating. Then, too, after an extended debate about this issue, that conversation might serve as a fair warning to whoever has leaked or might contemplate leaking in the future not to do it again, so the problem won't recur. Here in this group, the issue made everyone much more sensitive about keeping confidences, and people generally became more private about what they shared openly, and did more sharing off the list. The leaker was never discovered, but the problem never happened again.

# Today's Take-Aways:

 Be careful about what you share in a large and sometimes anonymous group, even if it is supposed to be a confidential support group. It may be less confidential and private than you think.

 Feel free to share about general topics in a large support group. But if the topic is personal or there could be a negative impact on your job, find a way to share it more privately and securely to be sure it stays that way.

Don't expect perfect confidentiality and privacy if you are in a nonprivate situation; despite the best of intentions and promises, things might still leak.

 And if something does leak that puts you in a negative light or harms a valuable relationship, think about what you can do to repair the damage.

 Regard the betrayal and the leak as two separate issues; treat the results of the leak as you would any other problem and figure out the best way to resolve it, leak or not.

# 18 Finders Keepers—*Or* Not?

What happens when you find some information you shouldn't know about in the workplace, but it could give you a big advantage if you can use it? Certainly, it's not legal to acquire information if you trespass in a private area, such as going through someone's desk or locker. It can be illegal to eavesdrop on a private conversation, particularly if someone is talking in his or her private office or you pick up the exchange on your cordless or cellular phone.

But what if you come upon the information in a perfectly legal way, such as when someone leaves an open folder on a desk in the conference room or posts a file in the wrong place on the company intranet, so others can access it freely for several days before he or she takes it down. Or suppose in doing a Web search, you find private information developed by a competing company that has been posted where anyone can access it, though certainly the company didn't intend to make this information public. What do you do? Should you use this information if it will help you or your company? Apart from the ethics of using it, what are the risks of using it if you get caught?

That's the issue that faced Sam, who had a job doing research for a marketing company. The company was involved in recruiting interviewees, facilitating focus groups, and writing up the results for its clients—and now it needed some funding to keep going, while it sought out new clients during an economic slowdown. Among other things, Sam was supposed to gather information for a database listing potential leads for investors, and such information was not easy to come by.

There were several directories he could access online, but he had to copy and reformat the data. The lists he could purchase from list brokers were already set up for mailing, but were fairly expensive. Meanwhile, the marketing company had a tight budget, and Sam knew his job was on the line if he didn't obtain the information quickly enough, so the company could start using it to contact potential investors.

Then in surfing the Web, Sam lucked into a bonanza. He found a Web page with a series of data files with the names of venture capitalists, contact information, and descriptions of the types of projects they were interested in financing. The files had been put online by another marketing company that was collecting similar information. Obviously, the information was not supposed to be released to the public generally, since there were no links to it from the company's main site. But the Web page turned up in the course of an ordinary Google search. The average person surfing the Web wouldn't find it if he or she took the first dozen or so links that turned up in a search. But Sam knew how to put in a series of terms to narrow the search and then had checked out the first 50 links listed, and one led him to the databases posted on the other company's site. So he hadn't hacked in or done anything illegal to get there.

Now that he had this information, what should he do? Should he use it or not? Even if he could use it legally, what about ethically? Could there be any problems down the road if he did?

# What Should Sam Do?

Here are some possibilities. In Sam's place, what would you do and why? What do you think the outcomes of these different options would be?

 Keep quiet about the information he has found, so he won't be under any pressure from Ted to use it, since this is private information and no one should use it.

Tell Ted about the information he discovered, but refuse to do anything with it once he hears the lawyer say they shouldn't use the other company's data.

 Realize that Ted's idea of cleaning and testing the data and then combining it with other data is the smart thing to do.

 Quit his job, because he is being told to engage in actions that are ethically questionable, and could have legal consequences if discovered.

 Send an anonymous e-mail to the other company telling them their data is exposed on the Internet and not do anything with it himself, including informing Ted that it is there.

 Other?

In this case, Sam first went to his boss, Ted, to help him decide. But Ted wasn't sure either, although he felt if the information was out there and anyone could use it, why not use it, too? "After all, if they're so dumb to post it on a Web site that anyone can access, it isn't confidential information any more, is it? And there's no copyright on the information in a list. So why not use it, if we can, especially if it will save us thousands upon thousands of dollars, which will help our company to survive." Then, Ted praised Sam for his great work in uncovering this Web site treasure trove of information.

So Sam headed back to his office, thinking that Ted's assessment made practical sense and was ready to make use of the data. But then Sam realized maybe there could be some way their competitor might realize they had used their information, such as by seeding the list with a few of their own names, so they would get any mailing. Then, if they did, they would know.

At once, Sam realized the potential danger. What if the other company found out? Could they retaliate legally or otherwise? Accordingly, the next step was consulting the company lawyer. His assessment: you can certainly compete by contacting the same venture capitalists, but just don't use the other company's data. The problem? Even though Sam had acquired the information legally and the company couldn't copyright the information itself, there could be a potential charge of unfair competition or the use of trade secrets, possibly resulting in a lawsuit should they find out.

But what if they didn't? And what if there was no way to prove they did? That's what Ted suggested their strategy should be, and so he directed Sam to examine the database closely, along with the company's Web site, to look for any listings that might be private ones belonging to those in the company and take them out. He suggested doing a test mailing after that using an e-mail from one of the free services, where you can create an e-mail account within minutes and sign up under any name you create. Then, if the test was successful and no one questioned receiving the mailing, they could use the data for a real mailing in the future, and they could eliminate anyone who raised questions from the data. "And no one will have the slightest idea who we are," said Ted.

Finally, Ted recommended using that database to get started, and then Sam could integrate other data from the online directories and lists. "This way, the data you have will be enough to get us started. Then, when we incorporate the other information, it becomes our own database with information we have gotten from multiple sources. And it's information that comes from many different places, so there's no way to claim we took someone else's database."

So with Ted's blessing, Sam checked over and used the other company's database to get started, and after testing he combined it with other data. The results? Very successful when the company found a venture capital firm to provide the additional funding it needed to maintain and later expand it's business. Sam got a raise and promotion, too, though sometimes he wondered later on whether he had in fact done the right thing. Was he right to feel twinges of conscience? Had he violated any ethical principles? Or was he just being old-fashioned, since Ted's strategy had proved very successful. There had been no legal challenge and the other company never found out, so the strategy passed the practical muster. But was it the right thing to do? Sam was never quite sure, and eventually his conscience stopped bothering him, since nothing can quiet such qualms as well as success.

What should you do if you are in a similar situation where you have access to valuable information and have gained that access quite legally, although there may be some ethical questions about whether to use it? Perhaps a big issue to consider here is your own ethics and the situation itself, because people have many different ethical approaches. These range from those who feel they have to do everything by the book and follow traditional morality to those who feel it is appropriate to make or break the rules and value doing what's pragmatic over following particular moral principles. Then, too, what system is appropriate can depend on the particular situation.

For example, in a competitive business environment, it doesn't always work very well to apply the same ethical system you might follow with friends, family, or close business associates to dealing with competitors, or you will get creamed in the real business world. In fact, some companies hire specialists in corporate espionage as a way to get ahead, and you don't hear about those who gain their behind-the-scenes intelligence quietly and successfully. So sometimes to survive or thrive you may need to consider more practical and strategic options that you might not want to use with a close friend or mate. After all, the business world is like being on a battlefield and arming yourself as if going to war if you are truly seeking to win. Sometimes you may have to shoot if you have the opportunity, rather than taking no action and getting shot yourself. As an example, think of Microsoft versus Netscape. Microsoft eventually won the browser wars by taking advantage of every opportunity that presented itself; it didn't worry whether doing so was the "gentlemanly" thing to do.

Thus, if you find yourself with a sudden advantage you didn't expect, use it if you can. Don't do anything illegal or anything that can get you in trouble or discovered by others. But if it's practical, think about how you can seize the moment. If someone else's mistake or release of useful information gives you an opportunity, why not use it? That's what generals and soldiers on the battlefield do all the time. So why not do the same at work or in business. If it's a winning opportunity with little risk of losing, go take it to win.

# Today's Take-Aways:

 There are no absolutes, even when it comes to moral and ethical considerations. Sometimes there are just wars when it comes to work and business issues, too.

 There's a difference between what's ethical and what's legal. While ethical and moral ideals may come into play in a particular situation, sometimes it pays to do the legal and practical thing.

 Different people have different definitions of what's ethical, so what's right to one person may not be to someone else; and what one person sees as ethical another may see as not the smart thing to do.

 Do you want to be right or successful? Sometimes what's "right to do" is what's ideally "right." In other cases, what's "right to do" is what's practical, because the world of work and business is sometimes like a battlefield. So you have to think like a general to win.

# 19

# Fraud
# Happens

Commonly, you don't think a trusted friend or associate is going to defraud you. You think if you feel close to someone, trust that person with personal confidences, and act in a spirit of good will to help him or her, particularly through a difficult period, he or she will reciprocate in kind. Well, yes, usually, that's the case. So we learn to trust and think our helpful actions will be appreciated and evoke a like response from others. We even have terms to express these ideals, such as: "You get back what you put out," "What goes around comes around."

However, those ideals also make it easy for someone who is a con artist at heart to take advantage of you, especially when you lay down your defenses out of trust and a desire to be helpful. In fact, that willingness to trust and believe people are who they say they are has opened the doors to the so-called social engineers, who talk their way into getting confidential company information and perpetrate big-bucks scams. Usually, such scams result from short-term encounters, even seeming business friendships that develop on the phone, such as the personable financial analyst with a get rich for sure investment scheme. Then, when the scheme collapses and people discover the truth, they may feel duped and taken advantage of. But they don't usually experience the intense sense of deep personal betrayal that comes from building up a long-term close relationship. Very often they feel ashamed, embarrassed, and guilty at having being tricked. But the personal betrayal is far more devastating, since it undermines bonds of closeness and intimacy, too. So how do you protect yourself from such a betrayal? Or how do you deal with if it happens to you?

That's what happened to Annette, a small gift products company owner, when she took Sarah, a new employee, under her wing. She met Sarah at a local business networking group, where she had been on a panel discussing how to develop sales leads for any type of business. Afterwards, Sarah spoke about how she had just arrived in town, and Annette felt an immediate bond with her, because they had both overcome some early challenges—first as teenagers overcoming learning disabilities and then escaping bad marriages to strike out on their own. Usually, Sarah didn't speak so openly about personal matters, but she found Annette so personable and engaging that she felt an immediate sense of trust. Annette also felt protective after learning that Sarah had been downsized out of a sales job for a home furnishing company when it experienced hard times. So Sarah had come to the West Coast to start a new life.

The upshot of the meeting was that within a few days, Annette offered to let Sarah stay in her spare bedroom while Sarah got settled. Annette even let her use her car and phone. Then, a week later, after Sarah still hadn't found a job, Annette invited her to do a project for her company that involved making corrections to update a file of sales leads she had gathered. "You just have to enter those corrections in the new information system," Annette explained. Annette said she couldn't pay Sarah very much, but figured that Sarah would appreciate the extensive help she had given her by opening up her home to her and so would be agreeable to being paid what Annette might otherwise pay a part-time student. Seemingly Sarah agreed. "Sure," she smiled. "I'll be glad to help out." So Annette gave her all the files.

Then, over the next few weeks, Sarah presumably made the corrections, using Annette's phone in a spare room turned into an office. Every few days Sarah described what she had been doing, and Annette paid her, thinking everything was fine, until finally Sarah said she had finished the project. She handed Annette all the files and said she had found a regular job, though she still needed a few more days to move to her own place. Then, with much thanks, she told Annette how truly helpful she had been. "Great," Annette said, thinking everything was fine, and pleased at how she had been able to help someone who had become a true friend.

But when Annette got her phone bill a few weeks later, she discovered several hundred dollars in calls back East. That same day, she received a notice from the court stating that she had two unpaid parking tickets about to double in price unless they were paid. Annette was stunned and immediately confronted Sarah about the phone calls and parking tickets.

"But you said I could use the phone to look for jobs," Sarah protested, though the phone calls were not for local area job calls. Besides, Sarah claimed, "I don't know anything about the tickets."

Then, in the morning, Sarah was gone, leaving a note that she was going to stay with a friend she had met. As Annette stared at the note, she felt upset and betrayed, feeling Sarah had taken advantage of her kindness and help. But the worse was yet to come. When Annette looked at the files of sales leads that Sarah had supposedly corrected and entered into the information system, she found that Sarah hadn't done anything at all. So not only was she four weeks behind in getting the work done, but she had paid Sarah, as well.

The experience left her shaken, wondering if she could trust anyone, and she spent dozens of extra hours herself to do the work Sarah hadn't done. Plus Annette had about $500 in extra bills to pay. For a time, she considered suing Sarah, but concluded "What's the point?," thinking that Sarah would probably not have any money to pay her, even if she won. Nor did she want to relive the experience in putting together her case. Rather, Annette decided simply to move on, though the incident left her feeling a loss of confidence not only in others but also in herself because she had been so wrong in befriending and deeply confiding in someone she thought she could trust.

# What Should Annette Do—or What Should She Have Done?

Here are some possibilities. In Annette's place, what would you do and why? What do you think the outcomes of these different options would be?

 Make sure it is clear what you are offering to do to help someone, such as stating that the phone is only for local calls.

 Ask Sarah to sign a written contract stating what you are offering and what she is promising to do.

 Ask more questions about what Sarah says she has done, and ask to see the records to make sure she has done it, before giving her the job.

 Spend some time with Sarah to watch her do the work to see that she is doing it correctly.

 Take Sarah to court even if there isn't any money now; if she is so good at conning people, she'll probably have money in the future, and since she may not show up, you'll win by default.

 Take more time to check out people in the future, regardless of how charming and trustworthy they seem to be.

 Other?

Probably in this case, moving on was the best thing Annette could do in order to put the incident behind her. There was little point in suing, not only because Sarah might not have the money, but because of their close personal connection. Since Sarah had been living in her house, Sarah might easily claim this was just a misunderstanding about what she had permission to do. And Sarah might have come up with her own slick convincing story about how she had done some work for Annette, so this was another misunderstanding, too.

Unfortunately, Annette's big mistake had come early on, when she was too quick to trust and then combined her personal relationship with a business relationship. Thus, she let her personal ties overcome her business sense, so she hired Sarah without the usual checks that she might have employed in hiring someone she didn't know. Then, too, because she was very busy and placed too much trust in Sarah, she didn't carefully check on what Sarah was doing—just relied on her descriptions every few days of what she had done. But Annette didn't think to spot check what Sarah said she had done to make sure that not only had she done it, but also had done it right. As a result, she left the door open for Sarah to get away with not doing anything. Certainly, had Sarah been skilled and not a con artist, such trust in a new friendship might have worked out fine, and the employment arrangement might have worked out well, too.

But the problem is that when you enter into a relationship so quickly, you just can't know. Someone could turn out to be a great friend, employee, partner, or other business associate, but you can't be sure so soon. Thus, it's best to let a relationship develop more slowly and use some checks along the way to make sure everything is as the other person says it is. This careful process is especially critical when you combine both the personal and professional, since you can lose doubly should things go wrong, as happened with Annette. Sarah not only betrayed their friendship and took money from Annette, but she committed a fraud against Annette's business as well both in taking money and falsely claiming she did work she didn't do.

Yes, it may feel uncomfortable to check out someone who you think of as a friend or have a close relationship with. But remind yourself that business is business, and perhaps explain to the person that this is your policy; that it's something your accountant or lawyer requires; or provide some other explanation to smooth the way. Then, check before you hire as you would any other new employee—do it yourself or use a pro to check for you. Today, you can't always be sure that people are who they say they are, especially when someone new comes into town. Just remember, con artists can con you because they are so personable and charming. So check carefully—and as in most relationships, take time to let it develop, since you are less likely to lose your money or your heart, or both.

# Today's Take-Aways:

 Before you can fully trust people, you have to know who they are, and that takes time.

 Don't rush the trust process and give up too much of yourself too quickly; take the time; otherwise someone could "take" you.

 To take the con out of con artists take the time to get to know someone and learn what she is all about. You might see her in a new and much brighter light that shows who she really is.

 Before you trust someone with both yourself and your business, make sure he or she deserves your trust.

 Do some checking before you starting writing checks to be sure the person you are checking on checks out.

# PART IV

# People Who Ask Too Much

# 20

# The Great Communicator— Not!

Sometimes people who think they are great communicators aren't, but that's not something they want to hear. They think they are clear and concise. When someone else doesn't understand what they said or makes a mistake following their instructions—well, it's because the other person should have understood or he got it wrong. Their problem is like that of the person who doesn't know and doesn't know he doesn't know. As one researcher reported in a study, the people who were clueless *were* clueless they were clueless. That's why they were poorly informed—they were unaware they didn't have the knowledge and acted as if they did.

Jimmy discovered this problem first-hand, when he was assigned to work on a series of research projects with a senior co-worker, Dan, who was designated as the team leader. Dan gave Jimmy some general in- structions for writing up his research findings, telling him to "echo back" what he found in other research reports. "Just mirror it back," Dan ex- plained, when Jimmy asked him to clarify what he meant.

After Jimmy wrote up the first page of his report, he asked Dan if he wanted to review it, but Dan told him: "Just send me the whole project when you're done." However, when Jimmy did as instructed, Dan complained Jimmy had written too much, since by echoing back, he had just meant Jimmy should summarize and paraphrase. "So now," Dan said accusingly, "the project is going to be much more expensive than projected." When Jimmy protested that Dan had turned him down when he offered to send his first page for review, Dan looked at him blankly. "What do you mean? You didn't ask me that." Jimmy was surprised, wondering if Dan had forgotten what he had said.

After that, Jimmy experienced further communication breakdowns, and he noticed problems that Dan had with other people, too. One time Dan assigned him to do some library research, and after Jimmy reported spending three hours on the project, Dan told him: "Keep going and keep me posted on the progress." So Jimmy did, submitting a few pages as a report every few days. At the end of one conversation, he commented that he had spent about eight hours to date. But when Jimmy turned in his last report which formally listed his hours, Dan blew a fuse. "How did this suddenly get up to 24 hours?" Dan yelled. "You put in too many hours and didn't tell me." Though Jimmy protested he had told Dan, Dan was equally firm: "No you didn't. I would certainly remember that."

Another communication breakdown occurred when Dan told Jimmy to present the research findings in a brochure with a certain design. But when Jimmy did so, Dan objected to the design, saying: "It's not professional enough. Do it again." So Jimmy did, working overtime to complete the task.

Then Jimmy began to notice that other members of the team were having similar experiences—misunderstandings about what to do, claims that their work wasn't right, requests from Dan to redo work even though they had spend the weekend doing it. Yet Dan was in charge. So Jimmy tried to do his best without saying anything, though he felt a growing resentment that Dan repeatedly blamed him for things that weren't his fault, and whenever he tried to point out the communication problems to Dan, Dan charged him with not listening, understanding, or remembering. Thus, after awhile, hoping to keep his job, Jimmy stopped protesting and sucked in his feelings, not wanting to rock the boat.

# What Should Jimmy Do?

Here are some possibilities. In Jimmy's place, what would you do and why? What do you think the outcomes of these different options would be?

 Ask for further step-by-step clarification of what Dan, the team leader, wants.

 Write up a memo of your understanding of what to do after each meeting or telephone conversation, and send it to Dan.

 Ask Dan to send you a written memo with instructions before you do the work, and explain you want this so you'll clearly know what Dan wants.

 Talk to others who have similarly gotten unclear communications and approach Dan as a group to discuss the problem.

 Write up a memo about what you have done each day and send it to Dan. Even if he doesn't read it, you could still use it to defend yourself to higher-ups in the company, if he tries to fire you or if you end up in court.

 Other?

What should you do in a situation like that, where you find yourself working with and getting directions from a person who thinks he or she is a good communicator, but isn't? Apart from walking away from the situation by quitting the job or the client, a good strategy is to press for clear communications. For example, send a memo or e-mail writing up your understanding of what you are supposed to do. If you think a job or project description is too vague or could have more than one meaning, feed back what you understand you are doing in different and more precise words. Try breaking down a broad description of a job or task into the particular steps you plan to do, and state what your plans are to see if they are correct. Importantly, too, seek feedback when you start on a project, even if the other person says that it's not necessary. For instance, say something like: "I realize you don't think it's necessary to see the project until I'm finished. But I can do better job for you if you let me know if I'm doing the right thing now." Then, hope the other person will agree to take a look. Alternatively, diplomatically seek out another source of the information and directions. You may not be able to fix all the communication problems with a supervisor or client who doesn't want to face his or her own problems in communicating. But you'll at least reduce the number of communication breakdowns and find fewer communication potholes on a sometimes rocky communications road. Plus you'll be covered by written documents showing your understanding of what to do if you get called on the carpet and have to defend yourself to others later on.

# Today's Take-Aways:

 People who think they are good communicators may not get the message when you try to tell them they are not.

 To improve communications with a poor communicator who's clueless, put up more signs with clearer directions to guide the way.

 Slow down and stop for feedback to help light your way and find the right road.

 Put your understanding of your instructions in writing in an e-mail or memo so you show what you know—or don't, and invite the other person to tell you if anything isn't right. Then, it's clear whose wrong when things don't turn out right.

# 21

# Learning *to* Let 'Em Go: *The* Demanding Client

Y ou've probably heard the expression from the popular song "The Gambler": "You've got to know when to hold 'em; You've got to know when to fold 'em." Well, you've also got to know when to "let 'em go." In other words, know when to stop the game or walk away—in relationships, not just in cards or financial deals.

That's what one of my clients—let's call her Susan—discovered when a long-term social relationship that evolved into a work relationship broke down. Susan, an administrative assistant in a big company, got used to seeing Anna socially at parties, at an after-work pub, and at occasional Chamber of Commerce mixers. Soon they were friends, talking about personal experiences and parties, and Susan told Anna about her plans to develop a career doing public relations and advertising, initially alongside her current work. A few months later, when Anna, who worked as a training consultant, hoped to start a training program for executives and managers on motivating and rewarding employees, she hired Susan to help her with the marketing campaign.

At first, the relationship seemed like a match made in heaven. When Susan presented her PR and marketing ideas and wrote marketing copy, Anna raved about them. She used superlatives like: "You're the greatest!" "You've got a real gift!" and "You write that so fast and well!" Between conversations on marketing and PR, they also took time to chat about the latest parties and gossip. "I'll deduct that time from my billing," Susan said, never wanting to take advantage of the friendship they shared.

Over the next months, Anna became a more and more demanding client. She called Susan to ask for a few minutes of advice every now and then, and when Susan added these to the bill, Anna got angry. "You're nickel and dime-ing me. That's no way to treat your customers." So Susan backed down, not wanting to hurt both a client and a friend.

Another time, Anna had a rush project, and when Susan said she could do it in place of another project, thinking Anna would appreciate her effort, Anna yelled at her, saying: "Are you trying to make me feel guilty that you are giving up work for me?" "No, no," Susan protested, apologizing profusely to placate Anna's feelings. After all, they had been such good friends, and since Susan was just starting her PR–advertising career, she didn't want to make any mistakes to offend her first client.

You can probably guess where this is going. Again and again, Anna criticized something Susan was doing, and Susan tried to smooth over the relationship by apologizing and sometimes adjusting the bill. The climax finally came when Anna had still another PR deadline. After Susan gave up a weekend and worked hard to meet it, Anna complained of mistakes, which Susan thought were due to unclear instructions from Anna and an outside vendor Anna hired to assist on the project. But when Anna wanted to schedule a conference call to discuss exactly what went wrong with the outside vendor, Susan backed down. "Can't we just agree there were communication breakdowns and split the difference?" Susan suggested, not wanting to engage in extended recriminations over what happened. But Anna was insistent. "No. How can I pay you anything, if you won't discuss what went wrong?"

## What Should Susan Do?

Here are some possibilities. In Susan's place, what would you do and why? What do you think the outcomes of these different options would be?

 Send Anna a letter explaining your position and why Anna should pay.

Tell Anna exactly what you think went wrong, including all the ways you feel Anna's own actions were unreasonable.

 Discuss the unclear instructions and outside vendor problems as diplomatically as possible, since this is what Anna wants.

 Give Anna a credit for the $1000 and hope for the best next time, since you don't want to lose the money and friendship, and every business has to put up with some difficult clients.

 Decide what's more important—keeping Anna as a friend and giving her the benefit of the doubt again, standing up to her whatever the consequences, or ending both the friendship and the business and moving on?

 Other?

For a moment Susan considered what to do; then finally said: "Well, then don't pay me at all."

She walked away, giving up about $1000 in income. Yet for Susan, leaving felt liberating. She felt like she had been trying to preserve the friendship and the new client relationship for too long. Again and again, she had given Anna the benefit of the doubt as the customer, since she (Susan) was fairly new to the field. She had deferred to Anna's criticisms and had let Anna define what was the proper way to treat a customer, even though she increasingly felt that Anna was asking for too much. Yet, afraid to confront Anna and threaten the relationship, Susan repeatedly backed down—until now.

Such scenarios happen again and again. You are new to doing something. You have developed a relationship with a friend, associate, coworker, or boss. You are afraid to rock the boat. You feel something is wrong in what the other person is asking of you, but aren't sure. You want to give someone the benefit of the doubt and show respect and deference. For whatever reason, you let a relationship that has lasted too long drag on.

When that happens, it may be worth it to simply walk away and let that relationship go. Whether you are firing a customer, breaking the ties with a friend, leaving that difficult boss or job, it's time to move on. You may have to experience some financial or psychic cost to do so. But in the long run, the act of disconnecting is worth it. It's time to simply LET GO!

# Today's Take-Aways:

 Don't get stuck holding on too long when the relationship is sinking.

 When you're in a leaky relationship, it's time to bail out—and then get out.

 If holding or folding isn't working for you, it's time to let go—and GO!

# 22

# *The* Give-*and*-Take Paradox

You probably know the give-and-take paradox very well. Regardless of your occupation, someone may ask you to use your skill to do something for him or her. Or you may ask someone to use his or her skill to help you out. The problem comes in distinguishing when you should help out or expect the other person to help as a favor, and when that help becomes a service for which you or the other person should get paid. What makes this give-and-take paradox so tricky is that different people have different views about where to draw the line between what they give freely and what they feel it fair to charge for. Different industries have different guidelines, too. Conversely, different people and industries have varying expectations about what to expect.

People in some professions, for example, are especially likely to complain about being hit by a brain drain when they meet people at social events. At a cocktail party a man says he's a lawyer, and people have all kinds of questions about whether they have a case and what to do about it. A woman introduces herself as a doctor at a reception, and people ask her to diagnose this or that symptom or give them advice on how to treat a problem. The professional may not really want to answer, but if he or she tries to cut off the questions or invites people to contact them later for a consultation—meaning "Pay me for my services," people often get offended. Given this dilemma, some follow a strategy of not revealing their profession, such as one career counselor, who never said what he did. "Otherwise the evening would turn into one long counseling session."

Often writers are particularly afflicted by this free-for-me problem, such as when friends and family members ask for free copies of their latest book. The people who ask think it's flattery to show interest, and they get offended if the writer is reluctant to give them a copy, sometimes because they think the writer gets the book for free or for a small amount, so why not give them a copy. But as one writer complained in an e-mail: "Why should you give away all that hard work for free? It's like asking someone in retail (who owns their own shop) to hand out free clothes. I'm willing to give them a discount, yes, but that's it."

Yet, the paradox of resenting it when others ask you for free information, services, or products because of a personal relationship is that you may resent it yourself when you ask others for free information, services, or products, and they say no. That's exactly what happened when one writer offered to sell other writers some PR lists of media contacts she had put together after spending about 100 hours and $500 on the project. Several writers strongly objected. One felt offended that the woman with the lists wanted to "sell, not tell." Another complained that she herself had spent a few hours researching a list of lawyers for another writer who needed some legal help. "And I wouldn't dream of asking her for any money," she exclaimed. Ironically, these are the same writers who object when others ask them for free books.

Thus, the big paradox is that we often expect free information, services, or products from others because of their personal or social relationship with us. Yet we don't feel it is right when others ask us to provide information, services, or products that we have to offer because of our special skills. Certainly, it's fine if you want to offer these freely. But if you don't want to do so, saying no should be legitimate, too, and likewise you shouldn't resent it when others resist a request.

# What Should Anyone Confronted by the Give-and-Take Paradox Do?

Here are some possibilities. What would you do when confronted by the give-and-take paradox and why? What do you think the outcomes of these different options would be?

 Diplomatically explain this is what you do for a living and invite the person to call you later if he or she still needs help.

 Don't tell people what you really do, so they won't ask you for free advice.

 Explain that you don't talk business in a social gathering and change the subject.

 Spend about two or three minutes helping the person as best you can in this time and showing off what you know; then give the person a card and invite him or her to contact you later for more help.

 Briefly offer some help; then give the person a flyer about the services you offer, should he or she need further help.

 Other?

In my view, the way to distinguish when it's appropriate to ask for and hope for freebies versus when it's appropriate to say no is to distinguish between what you or someone else does as a side activity—and what you or someone else does as a job or profession to make a living. If you do something as a hobby or sideline, rather than to make money, it's quite reasonable to volunteer your help or services and not expect to get paid. Likewise, it's reasonable to expect someone to help out you out freely if that activity is a hobby or sideline for them.

But once something becomes a profession or skill you use to earn money, that's a different situation. Then, it becomes reasonable to not give your work away for free and to find a diplomatic or lighthearted way to say no when friends, family, or social acquaintances ask. For instance, like the career counselor does at parties, kiddingly tell people you "are not on duty tonight," or like some writers, lawyers, and doctors do, offer friends and associates a discount on your products or services. Still another way of being diplomatic is to put off the conversation for now with a comment like: "I'd love to talk to you more about that. But I'd like to do so at a time when we can have a more serious conversation. Or if it's a product, you might say something like: "Why don't you give me a call in the office and we can talk about it then." Through such means you help to make a separation between dealing with an informal request for a freebie from a personal contact and handling this in a more serious or professional manner during your work time.

In any case, when such product or service requests in social situations occur, make it clear when you are relating to someone as a friend and when you are actually doing work, such as by stating when you are going to start doing some work for them. Or perhaps use a phrase like: "Okay, we're on the clock now, right?" to indicate what you expect and whether the other person agrees. This clarity can help make your relationship go more smoothly when you play two roles. If you keep the line fuzzy, misunderstandings and resentments often build up, such as when others think you should be doing something as a friendly favor, when you feel you have a right to expect to be paid.

Alternatively, if you are in a situation where you want help from a friend, family member, or social contact with a service, information, or product you want, be sensitive to how that person may feel when you ask for it. Don't put that person under pressure to say yes, when he or she may really want to say no. Yes, you may get something for free for now, but resentments are likely to grow. Rather, a good way to help preserve the relationship and keep the personal and work roles separate is to show your willingness to pay for that service, information, or product, or perhaps ask about any special discounts for friends and acquaintances. But then let the other person take it from there in offering what he or she feels is fair. This way you can better maintain the distinction between your personal and work relationships, and avoid the confusion and conflict that often result when you mix them up.

# Today's Take-Aways:

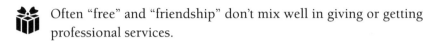 Often "free" and "friendship" don't mix well in giving or getting professional services.

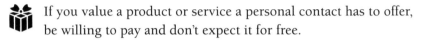 If you value a product or service a personal contact has to offer, be willing to pay and don't expect it for free.

If you don't want to give away a product or service to personal contacts who ask for it, don't feel guilty for wanting to say no. Instead, find a comfortable and diplomatic way to say this to keep your work and social words distinct.

# 23

# When Nothing Seems *to* Work, It's Time *to* Go Legal

S ometimes things simply don't work out. You've done everything
you can to solve a workplace problem as an employee, co-worker,
or boss. As an employee, you've repeatedly tried to explain, open up
channels of communication, apologize for perceived wrongs, clarify
what your boss wants, or otherwise improve relationships. As a co-
worker, you've tried to meet another employee more than halfway, but
still he or she disrupts your work and screams at you. As a boss, you've
tried to be extra diplomatic in telling the employee what he or she did
wrong and what you expect, and you've tried to be understanding in
listening to problems, but the excuses continue. Thus, nothing seems
to be working, no matter how many conflict resolution or problem
solving strategies you try and you are facing a workplace that might be
considered a hostile working environment or one that borders on harassment. So what then?

Unfortunately, there are times when you can't work out problems
through non-legal methods. Ideally, first do everything you can to reach
an amicable solution, taking into account your concerns and those of
the other party in the present situation. But after repeated failures, if you
think the situation is hopeless and feel it's time to give up, it may be time

to go legal—and that means getting strategic and tough. As they say, "choose your battles" so you don't end up fighting too much, particularly in hard to win situations. But once you decide to engage in a battle, do so to WIN—using the best strategy you can, whether you go it alone, turn to a union or trade association rep, or hire an attorney.

That's what happened to one woman who wrote me—I'll call her Doreen. She worked for a government agency and got promoted to another office, where her boss Teresa was missing a receptionist and under a lot of pressure. Doreen offered to help with that position as well as her own job, and Teresa was very appreciative. So the first months were fine.

But soon problems began mounting. Teresa would get off the phone with a client or even her husband and children and angrily slam the phone down. She frequently frowned at everyone, casting a pall of gloom over the office. She was also overly critical when Doreen had to take a week's sick leave for an operation. Then tensions mounted even more when Teresa hired a long-time personal friend, Judy, to be the receptionist. Judy was often away from her desk and made personal calls on work time, yet Teresa looked the other way out of friendship. So one day, Doreen wrote Teresa a letter about how the office could better use Judy to get more work from her, including helping her, so she could better do her own job.

The letter was like lighting a match to kindling to start a fire. As much as Doreen saw the letter as a diplomatic gesture, Teresa saw it as a challenge to her authority and went ballistic—screaming at Doreen, and after that, making her job a "living hell," by continually criticizing her, yelling at her, checking up on her, and giving her extra grunt work. So what should Doreen do?

## What Should Doreen Do?

Here are some possibilities. In Doreen's place, what would you do and why? What do you think the outcomes of these different options would be?

Send a more detailed letter to Theresa to explain the situation further and suggest some alternatives that might improve relationships and productivity in the office.

 Apologize again and show even more humility, to indicate how truly sorry you are and how much you want to work things out.

 Just work harder, even if it isn't fair, since eventually your hard work and silence will pay off, especially if Teresa has to fire her childhood friend and needs someone else who can do the job.

 Recognize that this situation can't be resolved easily, and start documenting all the ways in which Teresa mistreated you and Doreen messed up, so you can use this if you have to go legal.

 Find another colleague you feel close to, so you can share your concerns and feel more support to know someone else feels the same way.

 Other?

**M**y first suggestions to her were to try a mix of understanding and diplomacy. Maybe her boss had changed because of pressures on or off the job, making her more difficult to work with. Maybe Teresa's choice of hiring her childhood friend had backfired, putting her in a double bind of feeling loyalty to the friend, but finding her friend wasn't doing a good job. So she was reluctant to discipline her friend like a regular employee, felt guilty about this, and was taking it out on Doreen.

Thus, I suggested assorted "let's work it out" strategies, such as having a heart-to-heart discussion with her boss, during which Doreen might try to talk about what happened in a neutral conciliatory way to work things out. If it was hard to set up a meeting verbally, maybe Doreen could write a brief letter about how she hoped to work things out and point out how she and Teresa had once had a very good relationship.

Perhaps she could apologize if she had said some things she regretted or if there were lingering hard feelings about previous encounters. The discussion might also help clarify job responsibilities and expectations. Perhaps Doreen could talk to the receptionist who had been Teresa's childhood friend to work out a fairer distribution of work to take some pressure off her boss. Or maybe Doreen might find a co-worker who had a good relationship with both her and her boss to act as a go-between. Then, too, she might prioritize how much she wanted to stay there and work things out versus finding another job. In short, there were all sorts of routes Doreen might try to achieve a resolution.

However, as it turned out, though Doreen tried all of these approaches, nothing seemed to work. Her boss didn't want to talk about the problem; the receptionist wasn't interested in working harder; and her boss kept yelling and insulting her, culminating in a big blow-up when Teresa returned from a trip to visit one of her children who was having personal problems. Teresa came back to the office stressed out and began a tirade against Doreen, at which point Doreen gave up, contacted her union rep who advised her she had a case against her boss for harassment and permitting a hostile work environment to continue. So she filed a complaint against her boss for these causes of action and turned the matter over to her union to handle as a legal case.

Unfortunately, sometimes you do have to take some legal or official action when nothing else works. If so, it's a good idea to start preparing for this alternative once you think things might be hard to resolve, such as when your efforts to find an amicable resolution are continually rebuffed. Besides talking to a lawyer or union rep at some point if the problem continues, a key to this preparation is to document what has happened in an organized way, such as by keeping a daily dated chronology, in which you describe each incident in detail. This will help you both in presenting the situation to a legal adviser and to any legal action you may want to take down the road. Meanwhile, remain cool yourself to reduce any grounds for a legal counterattack. (After all, your adversary might be keeping a journal too.)

In the chronology, include the names of any witnesses to these events and contact numbers for easy follow-up. Any lawyer or grievance representative will ask you for such a chronology, and if you already have one prepared, this will help your case. At the same time, steel yourself so you are psychologically prepared to do battle, whether you remain on the job and fight it out there or you leave and afterwards seek compensation for damages. In addition, if this applies in your situation, look for other people who have been similarly affected, since they are potential witnesses or possibly victims in a multiple-plaintiff or class action suit.

Yet, even if you decide to go legal, it's best not to threaten any legal action while you are still preparing and gathering evidence, since positions will usually harden and anger will increase, making it harder to work things out. But once you are ready to go the legal route, play your legal cards to win.

In short, the first step should be to work things out. But if your efforts repeatedly fail, consider going legal, and if so, fight to win by preparing yourself with the documents and winning attitude you need for victory.

# Today's Take-Aways:

 As in war, so in the workplace. Do all you can to stay out of the battle; but once you enter it, fight to win.

 Before you go into a legal battle, get prepared both legally and psychologically—with documents and a positive "I'm going to win" attitude.

 As in poker, keep your plans to go legal to yourself until you are ready to act; then show your cards.

# 24 Passing *the* Responsibility Buck

**A** big source of problems in the workplace is when someone tries to pass the responsibility buck. It can be tempting not to pick it up when you can avoid it, since it's hard to admit a mistake even if only to yourself. Plus then you may have to face real consequences from shame to blame or worse. So you might find reasons why someone else should have done it, told you to do it but didn't, or told someone else to do it who didn't. Besides, you may tell yourself, "Why should I be expected to know?" and so it goes.

However, again and again, the failure to take responsibility and shifting responsibility for your own mistakes to someone else is behind breakdowns in group planning and action. A common result is a lack of follow-through and poor communication about whether something was actually done. Another fallout when someone doesn't take on his or her expected responsibility or tries to pass it on to others is that not only do things *not* happen, but people can get angry. In fact, read many books on leadership, and they all echo the theme—one of the keys to leadership is taking responsibility, as well as holding others accountable—a theme former New York Mayor Rudolph Giuliani emphasized in his own book, *Leadership*. Or as President Harry Truman put it on a prominently displayed sign on his Oval Office desk: "The buck stops here."

But what if you're trying to be responsible, but feel others around you aren't? Does that mean you'll end up getting stuck with all the bucks? That's not exactly like winning the lottery, is it?

That's what Ron began to feel when a colleague in a training company repeatedly looked to Ron to fix problems for him. The company was set up as a network of independent consultants, and it assigned the selected consultants to various projects. Then, consultants were free to bring in other consultants from the training company's network to help them on an assignment, such as to create a team-leading a workshop or to write materials for a client together. Generally, when one consultant asked for assistance, the administrative office would give an approval, put the assisting consultant on the payroll, and pay everyone once the project was concluded in about two to four weeks.

Ron had done a few assignments on his own without incident, but when he invited Tony, who had built a reputation in his specialty, to assist on a project, that's when the problems started, and Ron began to feel Tony was unfairly shifting his own responsibilities to him. Though Ron handled the bulk of the workshop, he felt that Tony's expertise would be especially helpful for a few sections of it. So, with company approval, he called him in. The program went well, and Ron was delighted, but about eight weeks later, he got an angry phone call from Tony, who was just back from six weeks of doing international workshops. Tony complained that he hadn't been paid, though he sent in his request per company policy. "So why don't you call the administrative department?" Ron asked. But Tony seemed irked by the question. "No. That's not my responsibility, and I really don't have time to chase down someone in payroll about this. It's your project after all."

For a moment, Ron thought, "But it's your money and your invoice." But not wanting to make any trouble, he sent out a few e-mails to his contacts in administration and payroll to check on Tony's invoice and see that he got paid. He pointed out that Tony was a well-known expert in the field, and he didn't want to antagonize him by late or lost payments, particularly since he might want to ask Tony to participate in one of his future programs. Within a few days, Tony was paid, though it bothered Ron that Tony had called and claimed he was responsible, when he should have easily handled the matter himself. "But it's no big deal," Ron told himself. "I did it for him, and it's done."

But then Tony started in a series of other demands, each small in and of itself, but part of a pattern of getting Ron to do something for him and claiming that Ron was responsible for doing it. For example, Tony had some questions about the attendees at the workshop that involved putting together a detailed list of information about them; another time he wanted additional copies of the outline Ron had used to lead the program, since he couldn't find his own copies and didn't have the time to make any copies himself from the master.

Though Ron was irritated, he complied, thinking it easier to do so than to make an issue of Tony's demands. But when Ron asked him to resolve still another problem, he began to wonder whether or not he should continue to take on what he thought were Ron's responsibilities. In this case, Ron had placed an order for instructional materials to use as handouts at his session, and since he was using some materials that Ron had developed, so that Ron received a small royalty for each sale, he asked Ron to help him find out what happened to his order, giving Tony the name of the client. "It's urgent," he concluded. "Otherwise, if the books won't arrive in time, it'll be too late for the seminar, and the client will cancel the order."

For several minutes, Ron gazed at Tony's e-mail, wondering what to do. Not only did Tony leave out some essential order information, like the order number, quantity ordered, costs, and shipping address, but Ron felt that Tony was again turning over another task that Tony should be doing. After all, it was Tony's order for his own client, though the tone of Tony's letter made it clear Tony thought that by rights Ron should be handling any follow-up.

By the time Ron came to me for advice, he was thinking it was time finally to confront Tony about taking on these responsibilities himself. He was ready to call or send him an e-mail telling him to take care of his own follow-up for payments and orders. Yet, was that the best thing to do?

# What Should Ron Do?

Here are some possibilities. In Ron's place, what would you do and why? What do you think the outcomes of these different options would be?

Tell Tony he's responsible for getting paid and getting the orders, and explain why so he understands.

 Tell Tony you're too busy to help him now and suggest how he can better take care of these matters for himself.

 Quietly take over Tony's responsibilities for now, since it doesn't take too much time or effort to do so.

 Do what Tony has asked to date, but have a conversation with him about future arrangements, so it's clear who's responsible for what.

 Other?

I n this case, a confrontational approach really wasn't the best one. Sure, Tony was not being fully responsible, since he should be taking care of his own invoices, payments, and orders. Even though Tony had gotten the assignment through Ron, that's where Ron's responsibility ended, much as if Ron had recommended a person for a job, who was then hired by another company to do it.

But even if Tony really should be responsible, it still made more sense for Ron to take care of the matter for Tony as a courtesy, since it involved minimal effort—maybe sending out a couple of e-mails or making a couple of phone calls to check on what happened to the instructional material Ron had ordered. Moreover, even though Tony might be shifting his own responsibility to Ron, Tony still had a powerful reputation in the field because of his expertise, so it didn't make sense to confront him over something that might take a few minutes of extra effort. Plus if a confrontation did make Tony angry, he might cancel his order for Ron's instructional materials, thereby reducing Ron's royalties, and he might be unwilling to assist Ron on his programs in the future. Ron quietly sent off a few e-mails to the order department to ask about Tony's order;

eventually, Tony's lost order was replaced with a new one. Sure, Tony could have and should have done it himself, though he didn't think he should. But here it made better practical sense for Ron to humor Tony and take over the responsibility for him, since the time and effort involved to do so was relatively minor, compared to the risks of standing up to him and trying to give that responsibility back.

Likewise, if you are in such a situation, it's good to take stock of what is going on before you act. For example, consider whether you should be responsible for something yourself or whether you are manipulating someone else into taking on that responsibility for you. If so, even if the other person does what you want, he or she may feel uncomfortable or resentful, even as he or she does what you want, much as Ron felt about Tony's requests. It's much better to appeal to the person to do you a favor, since you don't have the time or feel he or she might be better able to get results than to expect the person to take on what is really your responsibility.

Alternatively, if you are in a situation where someone is trying to shift his or her responsibility onto you, consider the situation strategically to decide whether it's worth telling the person where you feel the responsibility really lies or whether it might be easier to accommodate the request, even if unjustified. For example, if a request will involve a great deal of extra work, and you feel the other person is taking advantage of your good nature by piling on more work, then this is probably a good time to speak up (unless of course it's your boss making the demands or your job is at stake). Otherwise, if it might be easier to take on the extra responsibility for someone else, do so. Consider doing this as a kind of courtesy or as a means of following some commonly cited principles for getting ahead, based on "Going the extra mile" or "Delivering more than is expected." So even if someone else slacks off on his or her own responsibility, at times it makes sense to take up the responsibility buck for him or her. Sometimes there are advantages to picking up those extra bucks or the cost of not picking them up can be too high. Then, as you can, diplomatically let others know where you have played this responsibility pick-up game. It's a way of eventually cashing in your responsibility chips so you win even more.

# Today's Take-Aways:

 Don't pass on the responsibility buck if it's in your own wallet. Rather, hold onto the bucks you have, and you'll find a greater payoff in the future.

 If someone tries to pass a responsibility buck onto you, consider whether it's worth taking or not; then take it on if it's worth it to you.

 Sometimes it's best to view taking on someone's responsibilities as providing an extra service or courtesy.

When you feel resentment about taking on someone else's responsibility, consider how much they may appreciate it if you take it on and the possible conflict that can result if you don't do something. In other words, what's the cost of doing something versus the cost of doing nothing? When you weigh and balance them together, that's what counts.

# 25

# Get Out
# While You Can

Commonly, at the beginning of any new project or deal, you hope for the best and enthusiastically look forward to start working. You want to believe your teammates or partners feel the same, and you're open to giving someone the benefit of the doubt should problems develop. In fact, you may not even see these initial difficulties as problems—rather they are start-up "challenges," and you hope to do all you can to promote progress. Usually, that's the spirit to keep involvement, commitment, and motivation high. After all, if you start into something new with a huge dose of skepticism, you'll hold back, not get much done, and put a damper on everyone's spirits.

Yet, at the same time, keep an eye open for truly serious problems that are signs the project or deal is in trouble. That's when it pays to surface those issues, see if they can be resolved, and halt or even end the arrangement. In other words, proceed with enthusiasm, yet carefully observe and evaluate. You are essentially keeping your watchfulness on a shelf, where it can check on what's going on, without interfering with your participation. Yet if necessary you can always pull it off the shelf to say "Hold on," "Let's look at this," or "Get out and move on." Another way to think of this approach is that you are finding a balance—between participation and observation, between digging in and watching yourself dig, between your right brain's emotional excitement and your left brain's rational analysis of what's going on.

That's what Delores should have done when she entered into a new partnership with Jacob. She met him at a local business networking group, and her idea was to create some personalized craft items to sell on the Internet to individuals and retail stores doing e-commerce. She had only recently learned how to create Web pages after taking an introductory Front Page class, but Jacob impressed her, since he was at a small table by the wall pitching his Web design skills. He thought her idea would be a good way for him to expand his Web development business by getting into e-commerce himself. Plus he told her, "I love setting up databases. That's what I do. You just get the information you want to use and I'll put it in the database."

And so they set up a simple partnership agreement. Delores agreed to provide the information for the database and handle advertising and promotion, while Jacob would provide the Web site and software. Then, since Delores already had some lists of individuals and organizations she had spent several months gathering, they worked out a graduated agreement through an exchange of letters about how to distribute the partnership proceeds—60% to Delores for the first six months, 55% for the next six months, and 50% to each of them after that. Jacob said he would incorporate those percentages into the partnership agreement he would send to her.

Based on that understanding, Delores made some final updates to her lists of retailers and nonprofit organizations, calling to check on current names of owners, addresses, and e-mails. Then, she passed on the information to Jacob to enter into the database. But after Jacob entered her first list of retailers, he told her the entry was taking much longer than expected, and while he appreciated her effort in getting the list together, he felt Delores was getting too much if they started off at 60%. Instead, he wanted to start off with a 50–50 partnership. That would be "fairer" he said, and he would feel more comfortable with such an arrangement.

# What Should Delores Do?

Here are some possibilities. In Delores's place, what would you do and why? What do you think the outcomes of these different options would be?

 Call a halt to the arrangement early on when Jacob seeks to change the agreement. He isn't sufficiently valuing your own contribution.

 Agree that Jacob's request is reasonable and the fair thing to do.

 Discuss Jacob's initial request to change the arrangement more fully and work out a more detailed understanding of who is doing what.

 Insist on keeping the original agreement, even if that means ending the partnership at the outset. After all, a deal is a deal.

 Give Jacob the benefit of the doubt on his offer, since he has a clearer understanding of how much work will be involved in the future.

 Agree to the change, since you did do the work in the past and he's contributing the work to the partnership now and in the future.

 Agree to the 50–50 split, but tell Jacob he can't ask you to do more, and get out if he insists.

 Other?

His request sounded reasonable, and Delores wanted to do what was fair, so she agreed. Though she had spent hundreds of hours in the past gathering her material, she tried to see things from Jacob's point of view. She also felt dependent on Jacob, since he was the one with the Web skills. She believe she couldn't move ahead without him; and the thought of trying to find another partner, if she even could, was dismaying. So quickly and graciously, Delores agreed. "Sure. I'll agree if you think that's fairer," and Jacob faxed her the revised contract, which she signed.

But then, ever so gradually, Jacob started to make other requests that started changing what had been Delores's understanding of the agreement, so Delores kept doing more and more. Initially, using sales and advertising copy Delores wrote, Jacob had set up the Web site so that customers could place their orders and pay directly online. Then Jacob would process them and send Delores the payment confirmation, so Delores could send out the items with the client's name and picture. But some clients had questions. At first, Jacob responded to them as part of the order-taking process. But then he asked Delores to take care of this customer contact, since he didn't have time to do that and finish the Web site. So Delores agreed, spending an hour or two providing information directly to customers who couldn't or didn't want to find this information themselves in one of the pages already on the Web. Then, though Jacob had done the original data entry, he asked Delores to learn how to go the Web site, so she could enter new data herself. He quickly squashed Delores's initial objections. "It's really easy," he insisted. "Just go there and you'll see." Yes, it was. But it was also time consuming.

Then, when Delores got a few return e-mails from customers and forwarded them to Jacob, he immediately phoned to berate her, telling her: "In the time you spent sending me the e-mails, you could have gone to the online database and done the entry yourself."

So it went, until Delores felt she was doing almost everything now that the Web site and all the copy she had written for it was online. She was responding to the customer e-mails, gathering new information and updating the database, and writing and placing new promotional copy. So what was Jacob doing? Basically, sending out the order confirmations to Delores to fulfill, when an occasional order came in. But the process of taking on additional responsibiltiees had occurred so gradually that she didn't realize what had happened until one day, about four months into the partnership, she went to her banker to find out what was in the bank, since Jacob had not been sending her the monthly statements.

"I can't seem to do anything right," she complained, "and I don't have the time to do enough advertising and promotion, because I'm doing so much else." That's when her banker responded: "But you're the victim here. Your partner has been taking advantage of you, so you've been doing his work. He's defining your contribution to the database differently than you understood when you signed the contract. So now he's making you do it all."

That's when Delores suddenly understood. Gradually, she had let Jacob shift more and more responsibilities to her, and she had quietly accepted his reinterpretations of their respective roles in the partnership. He had made his requests to do more so gradually that she didn't realize how much more she was doing. Plus she had been hesitant to challenge him and rock the boat, since he knew so much more about all the technical and financial details of the business. She was afraid maybe he might even back out. She hadn't thought to consider whether it might have been better if he did or to examine other possibilities, such as her ability to learn to take over the few things he was doing now or her ability to find another partner.

In any case, Jacob's actions in passing on so many responsibilities to Delores helped doom the partnership, since she didn't have time to market and promote the business. Thus, few orders came in, and a few weeks later, Jacob announced that if the partnership didn't start getting in more orders and making a profit in the next few weeks, he would have to leave it anyway. He had other promising business offers now, and he would be glad to turn over his share of the partnership to her. But there was very little to turn over. The partnership was worth little to anyone, and Delores didn't have the enthusiasm and energy to continue the project on her own. And so it died.

Unfortunately, Delores's big mistake came early on in the partnership, though she didn't realize it until reviewing what happened in hindsight. Certainly, in many cases, a change in arrangements is in order, because as you proceed in a partnership you discover you are playing different roles and one may have more work to do, the other less. But sometimes a change in the rules can portend a dangerous road ahead when one person uses these changes to take advantage of the other. The critical difference is whether the rule change is fair and then whether the changes continue to seem fair or not. So it's important to monitor what happens after you make a change that seems appropriate at the time.

The first warning sign was when Jacob asked to change the terms of their partnership, and did so on a basis that devalued her own past work and contribution to the project and placed more value on what he was doing now. Another red flag was that he had entered the partnership by telling her how easy it was for him to do the work he did—the database entry, so it wasn't right for him suddenly to claim it was harder than expected and so get more. Still another cause for concern is that what Jacob was doing was a form of the classic nibble in financial and real estate dealings. He was asking for a little bit more, and after getting an agreement, asking for a little bit more after that. Here the deal was asking Delores to spend more time and do a little bit more in the business, while he did a little bit less, and since time is money, well, you get the idea. Delores's contribution to the arrangement kept going up and up, while his was going down. It wasn't the change in the rules that was the problem, but that the repeated changes led to an increasing imbalance in the work each did compared to the money they got. It was like they were two people on a teeter-totter, where as the one was weighted down with more and more work, the other rose higher and higher and got more and more benefit in return for what he was doing.

However, since Delores kept wanting to trust Jacob's judgment and give him the benefit of the doubt, she never thought to question him; she never thought to say stop or get out before she was further and further into the project. So as she kept contributing so much more time and energy, it kept getting harder and harder to pull the plug.

In a classic financial–real estate nibble, there's a one-time agreement and the nibble goes on until the contract is written which firms up the deal. But here, what made the situation even worse is that the nibbling continued on into the partnership, making the arrangement more like a classic case of domestic abuse, where the stronger partner (usually male) uses the other's dependency to gain more and more from the relationship, while the other (usually female) accedes to his demands and gains less and less, only to be "put in her place" and abused some more.

But the dependent partner doesn't realize this, as her own confidence shrinks and she depends more and more on her abuser. In effect, that was what was happening to Delores, as Jacob kept asking for more and she acceded. She gave him the benefit of the doubt each time and believed she had to continue the partnership because of her dependency on him. Her situation was much like the woman finding excuses to continue an abusive relationship, say for the sake of the kids, as the violence escalates. Generally, the best response in such situations is simply to get out now, while you still can, unless some effective outside intervention occurs, such as counseling to effect radical, healing change.

Likewise, if you enter into any agreement, watch for any signs that in changing the arrangement, someone is sucking you onto a teeter-totter where they become increasingly dominant and demanding, and you find yourself contributing more and getting less. A first sign may be a request to change the terms of the original agreement; other warning signs may show up when the other person asks for more and more. If that happens, a good initial response is to discuss fully any changes with a partner and carefully consider his reaction. If he's willing to discuss them and hear your concerns, that's a good sign; but if he acts dismissive, puts you down, or reemphasizes his own contribution, that's a warning to look more closely. When you do, seek to view the situation like a neutral third party rather than giving the other person the benefit of the doubt. How would an outside judge look at what's going on? Then if you feel the arrangement is becoming unfair and unbalanced, it's time to get it back into balance or to get out. Otherwise, the arrangement is likely to get more and more unbalanced, and you'll have more and more invested in the relationship and less and less power to regain that balance as time goes along.

# Today's Take-Aways:

 If someone tries to change an agreement claiming fairness, ask yourself what's fair from your point of view, not just his or hers.

It can be fine to change the rules when circumstances change. But don't let anyone use a rule change as a way to put you at an increasing disadvantage.

 Approach any new opportunity with enthusiasm and commitment, along with a dose of wait-and-see observation, so you can figure out if the changes really are reasonable and fair, and be ready to raise questions if you think they're not.

 Be both participant and observer, believer and skeptic, so you can keep your balance should things start to go wrong.

 If you encounter someone who nibbles, it could be a rat.

 The longer you stay in a trap, the weaker you'll get; so once you start to feel you are being drawn into a trap, get out then and there.

 When you start to get too dependent on someone, that's the time to step back and declare your independence. This way you turn your dependence into Independence Day.

# 26

# When Help Turns *into* Help!!!—Get Me Out *of* This

Sometimes the help that seems so useful can turn into more of a hindrance when someone tries to help too much. Then, rather than being helped and guided, you can feel controlled and led. The process can occur very gradually, and the path from help to hell can be paved with good intentions. But the net result is you end up feeling trapped and just want to get away. The trap seems so enticing in the beginning— you feel like you're getting a great tasting treat. However, in time, the helper turns into the hunter and you become their prey.

That's what happened to Marvin after he joined a company's training department. He began working on developing a training program for the customer service department, which had recently set up a call center with customer service reps in different areas of the country. His job was to create an online series of classes that these reps could access to learn what to do. His supervisor, Ann, provided his initial instruction on how to write these programs, which combined descriptions of techniques with role-play practice and take-it-yourself quizzes to see how you're doing. She then left him a detailed instruction manual, before flying across the country to work with other program developers at another office. Thus, Marvin was left pretty much on his own with the deadline she gave him, and as he wrote up his ideas for what to include in the program, he felt increasingly lost. Though he knew how to write, he didn't know what to say, since he was unfamiliar with call centers and the detailed manual only made him feel more confused. He wasn't sure what was important to feature and how to set up the role plays and quizzes.

Enter Fred, who at first seemed like a helpful savior. Fred, also in the training department, had been developing these programs for a year, so he knew how to write them, and he had even worked in a call center before. "So let me help you," he offered, after he heard Marvin complain in the office lunchroom that he felt lost.

Marvin was delighted for the support, and at first everything seemed fine. Fred showed Marvin an example of one of his own completed training programs, and gave him tips on how to phrase his questions and write up the role play practices. "Just imagine you are a call center operator, and think of various situations you might encounter when a customer calls," Fred told him. Then, Fred suggested a few scenarios Marvin might use, drawing on his past experience in customer service, so Marvin only had to write them up. When he was done, Marvin showed his program to Fred, glad for his help, and when Fred made a few suggestions for minor changes in the dialogue, Marvin quickly made them. After all, he figured, Fred must know more, since he's been here longer, though he thought the suggested changes were more a matter of style, such as making one of the characters in a scenario a few years older and more authoritative.

But then, as Marvin felt a growing confidence in what he was doing now that he had a model to follow, problems developed. Since Fred had expressed interest in seeing the next lessons that Marvin wrote up, Marvin continued to copy Fred when he sent off his lessons to the IT specialist, who was putting the programs he wrote online. To Marvin, copying Fred was a kind of courtesy, a way of saying "Thanks for all your past help." But Fred continued to give him feedback, suggesting additional changes—"to make it even better," Fred urged.

Initially Marvin complied, thinking yes, he did want to make his work even better, while at the same time, wondering if Fred's additions were really necessary. Yet, since Fred had been so helpful and knowledgeable in the beginning, he felt he should go along with Fred's suggestions for that reason; plus he felt if he turned down Fred's input now, Fred might be offended. Sure, some of Fred's advice was good, but Marvin wasn't sure he still needed it; he had developed his own style. So as the days went on, more and more he felt he was making changes to please Fred, not because they were necessary. And more and more, Marvin began to feel like he was doing the project under Fred's control and supervision; he had let his need for help and his eagerness to show his appreciation lead him into a trap.

Meanwhile, Ann, who had gotten copies of his work, said she liked what he had been doing and that she would be back in the office soon to discuss the current project and possible new ones. Her impending arrival made Marvin feel even more tense—like he had to decide now what to do about Fred and whether he should say anything to Ann about how he felt. After all, Fred had been so helpful once. Would it be like a betrayal of Fred if he complained now?

# What Should Marvin Do?

Here are some possibilities. In Marvin's place, what would you have done or do now and why? What do you think the outcomes of these different options would be?

 Talk to Ann when she returns, tell her about the problem, and ask her what to do.

 Have a heart-to-heart talk with Fred to tell him that you are uncomfortable with his continued help and find out why he has been going out of the way to help you so much.

 Tell Fred you appreciate his past help but feel you know what you are doing now, so you don't need any more help, without going into detail to explain why.

 Let Fred continue to give advice, but don't take it, so he soon gets the message you don't need any more help.

Avoid talking to Fred as much as possible, and eventually he'll stop offering suggestions, so the problem will eventually go away.

 Other?

**M**arvin may have many reasonable options, but his goal should be to end getting the no longer wanted or needed help from Fred as diplomatically and gracefully as possible. He doesn't necessarily need to find out Fred's reasons for wanting to continue to help either—in fact, making an issue of them could create an even more uncomfortable situation.

Fred might want to help for a number of different reasons. He could be angling to become a supervisor and is doing what he might do in this role after a promotion. He could be a person who feels a strong need to be needed. He could have a personal interest in Marvin and hopes that by helping he might kindle an off-the-job relationship. He could simply enjoy the feeling of power and control. However, in this case, trying to find out "why" isn't necessary. In fact, trying to find out why could open up doors you don't want to enter; it could lead you to places you don't want to go. "Why" can be like fishing in dark murky waters, and sometimes you can pull up all sorts of things from the bottom that are better left below, such as personal agendas that could prove embarrassing.

Bringing Ann into the mix might also contribute to escalating the situation, not a good choice since Marvin did initially get some very useful help that helped him gain Ann's praise for doing a good job. Ignoring the situation by seeming to play along with Fred but not using his advice or trying to avoid him could lead to misunderstandings, too. That's because the sudden change in Marvin's response to Fred could leave Fred puzzled and hurt, and Fred might initiate a confrontation with Marvin to find out what's going on.

Rather, probably the best approach is for Marvin to find some way to show his sincere appreciation for Fred's initial help—whether by giving him a heartfelt thanks or some small gift of appreciation, perhaps around the time of Ann's arrival. But at the same time, Marvin could quietly say that he feels additional help is no longer needed, since he knows what to do now. Then to add some honey to make the words of separation go down more smoothly he might ask if he can call on Fred's assistance in the future if needed. In short, this approach provides a gentle way to say "thanks" for what Fred did in the past and tell him "Maybe you can help in the future," but for now the sign says: "No help needed now."

Likewise, if you are in a similar situation with an overly helpful co-worker or colleague, be ready to accept the initial help if you need it. Why turn it down because you are worrying about what could happen in the future, since you really don't know what will occur? The person could simply proffer the help you need, then gracefully stop helping when you are ready to go on your own (unless this is part of a recurring pattern, and in that case it may be best to find an alternate source of help if possible).

But then, once you feel you don't need any further help, don't feel obligated to continue accepting it, whether you feel the person is knowl-edgeable or feel he or she might be hurt if you turn down an offer for help. Then find a comfortable, casual way to express your gratitude for the past help you have received and indicate that you hope you might be able to ask for help again in the future if necessary, but for now you don't need any more. In most cases, that should be a supportive, non-threatening way to end the problem—showing appreciation at the same time that you pull back.

# Today's Take-Aways:

 Don't let help turn into hell!!! If you feel someone is helping too much find a gentle way to say thanks for then, but now no thanks.

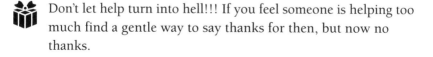 When someone tries to help you too much, he or she could have a multitude of reasons, but you don't need to know them—and often it is better not to know or try to find out.

Think of help like a lifeline—it's great when you need it, since it can pull you out of a tight spot. But if the lifeline gets too long, it can turn into a rope that can strangle you.

 Too much help can turn into a trap that keeps you stuck and dependent on the helper, who can becomes like a captor or jailor. So if you fall into the trap or see it closing in on you, get out as quickly as you can. Leave the palace before it turns into a prison; turn the knob on the door to leave before the handle comes off or you lose the key.

# PART V

# Capturing
## *and* Keeping
### *the* Job

# 27
# Beating *the* Recommendation Game

A big problem today is getting recommendations, especially when the company you have worked for is no longer in business or the person you worked for has moved on. In high-tech towns this is a particularly critical problem, because so many companies have disappeared and so many layers of supervisors have collapsed like a house of cards, leaving no one around to give a referral. Even when companies and personnel are stable, getting recommendations can still be like prying information out of a locked vault, because so many employers have become recommendation shy, so they will say little more than dates of employment, job title, and possible salary. Why? Because if they say anything negative, even if true, they fear they could be sued by the employee who is looking for a job. Or if they don't say anything negative and the employee messes up on the new job, they could be sued by the new employer for giving a recommendation that contributed to hiring the employee who caused the damage.

Well, you get the picture. In our lawsuit-happy society, people fear to say anything, even when they are still around to say something—which isn't that often.

Unfortunately, this "no recommendation" stance can create many problems for the person trying to get a job, since many prospective employers still insist on references. As one reader—let's call her Susan—

who had been running into difficulties for five years explained in an e-mail: "The most recent written job reference I have is from five years ago. I've asked supervisors since then to write references, but they declined, citing company policy." Then, Susan went on to explain that when she gave out the name, address, and phone number of her last supervisor, he would only give out the barest of information about her job title and the dates she worked there. She struck out with several other previous employers, too—her next most recent employer had left the state; another one had retired; and a third who had given her a letter had left the company and no one knew where he had gone.

Now Susan's dilemma was that a potential employer wanted to chat personally with one of her former supervisors about her job performance, but she had no one to do this, and she felt she was repeatedly losing out for jobs she was qualified for, because she lacked the right references. So what should Susan do? Or what should you do if you are having trouble getting the references you need?

# What Should Susan Do?

Here are some possibilities. In Susan's place, what would you do and why? What do you think the outcomes of these different options would be?

 Make such a good impression with your resume and other references that a recommendation from this elusive employer doesn't matter.

 Find someone else other than your supervisor on your previous job who can give you a reference.

 In lieu of a reference, offer to work on probation for a day or two so your prospective employer can see how good you are.

 Get general letters of reference before you leave a job—and even offer to write up a letter for your boss's review.

Take some stationery before you leave the job and write up your own reference if your former boss is gone, since he can't be found and this is what he would have said anyway.

 Collect together anything you can—from reference letters on previous jobs to awards and citations—that show what a great job you have done for others, even if you can't get this particular reference.

 Other?

Given the realities of the current jobs market—companies disappearing or downsizing, supervisors and managers moving on, employers fearful of saying the wrong thing—the reality might be that you just can't get these references. If so, look for alternative solutions, so a prospective employer feels comfortable using other information about you to feel confident making the hire.

A good way to start is by doing everything you can to make a bang-up impression with everything else you have to offer, so the references become less important when they do come up. For example, take extra care to have a super-good resume; get references from community leaders or volunteer program supervisors who know you (and get to be known by them if they don't); prepare to do an extra good interview, so you can appear to have great confidence and expertise. If appropriate, get a reference from a supervisor in another division who knows your work or a colleague still with the company, though such references aren't always possible. Incidentally, while one of the listed possibilities was to take some stationery and write your own reference on office stationery, this is very definitely not something to do. Besides being dishonest and unethical, your fraud could be discovered later, such as after you do find a job based on your misrepresentations, and you could quickly be out of another job, with even worse prospects of finding another one.

To help with your preparation, say affirmations to yourself, such as: "I don't need my references to get hired," "I will get the job I want without any references," so you let go of the feeling and belief that you need the references.

Whenever a request for references does come up, be immediately up front about why you don't have them. If you are talking about one or two jobs you have held for a long period of time, you might easily explain this verbally. Or if you have had a number of jobs where this is a problem, create a written bullet-point list for each job, along with the name of the company, supervisor, and what happened, to explain why you don't have a written reference letter or why your previous supervisor can't be contacted. Certainly, a prospective employer should be able to understand and accept why his or her request for references can't be fulfilled, if you present it clearly and confidently.

The next step is to offer some alternatives that a prospective employer might accept as a substitute if he or she wants some further performance evaluation of how you do on the job. For instance, offer a recommendation from a community leader or volunteer program leader who has seen you in action. Also, prepare for providing this additional information by keeping files of materials you might use, such as copies of performance reviews or memos praising your work. Preferably keep your collection of kudos and support at home in organized files, so you can readily access this information when you need to—and don't have to worry about not being able to get it from your workplace, say if you are suddenly fired or laid off.

Still another possibility in lieu of strong references is to make a-hard-to-refuse proposal to show your keen interest in the job and to show the prospective employer how you perform first hand. How? You might say something like: "Let me work for you for (a day, two days, a week, whatever seems reasonable) to show you what I can do. If you like my work, hire me; if not, you have no obligation to so. But I'm so sure you'll like what I do, that I'm willing to take the chance and work for you on this no-obligation basis."

In short, if you can't come up with references, come up with alternatives. Use these to show you'll be great in the job, and why your prospective employer doesn't need any references—either written or verbal—to show how great you will be."

# Today's Take-Aways:

 If you come up against one closed door, look for another door that will open. If references won't work, find an alternative that will.

 Getting references is like getting sodas from a vending machine. If you can't get one soda, try another—and maybe it'll taste just fine or even better.

 Don't let getting no references get you "NOs." Instead, find other types of references to turns all these "NOs" into "YESs."

 Keep an organized file or library of files of anything you might use to show your credentials. Then, you're always ready when you need to do an office show and tell.

# 28
# Knowing When *to* Back Off: Don't Push *a* Negotiation Too Far

Sometimes it's better to back away and take what you have, rather than trying to ask for more. Even if you aren't sure you have made the best possible deal, *a* deal may be better than *no* deal. Pushing your luck can push a good deal right off the table. That's particularly so when you make a deal after extended negotiations and later remember what you forgot to ask for or face an unexpected contingency. It may be better simply to back off, though you think your request for more is only fair. But the other party may suddenly see you as a difficult person to deal with since you are making still another request; hence the end of the deal.

You might compare this situation to the "nibble" in a real estate or other sales negotiations. You think you have reached an agreement, when the other party comes back with an "Oh, by the way," then asks for a little bit more. You may feel angry and want to walk off, and sometimes people do, while others may reluctantly give in, willing to make one last concession, yet angry all the same. Unfortunately, that's what someone else may feel when you ask for that little bit more in that you think you deserve it. But the other party may consider your request a deal killer and walk away. Even if you are asking for a small additional amount, your after the agreement request can cause problems, because once you make a deal, the other party may be thinking: "This is done. I can move onto the next thing." But then you come back asking for changes, and the other person can suddenly think you might be a difficult person to work with and they just don't want the hassle. So while they might have agreed to the additional amount at an earlier point in the negotiations, now is not the time to ask for more. The request backfires and blows the deal. And you get zero, instead of more. This kind of dynamic works in sales agreements—and when you're trying to get a job or negotiate with a business client.

That's what happened to Sidney. He was trying to nail down a job doing PR for an out-of-town company in the Northwest that was having a financial slowdown. After offering him a two-year contract for a job, the company had to cancel it, giving him a few thousand dollars to cover his signing and moving expenses, since he had already put up his house on the market and had to pay off the buyer when he backed out of the deal. Then, about two months later, their financial problems over, the company's Human Resources director offered him the job again, and Sidney agreed. Though he tried to ask for a slightly higher salary, he encountered some resistance, since he had been willing to accept less before, so he quickly backed down. But he did get a commitment for at least six months of work, to make it worth his while to put his house on the market and move. After the contract arrived, however, Sidney saw that the company president wanted him to agree not to do any PR work, even if it was noncompeting work on his own time, and he expressed some concerns about that. At this point, the HR director told him the company president was getting upset about the negotiations, and he could either sign the contract or not. And so he did. Afterwards, he proudly told his friends, neighbors, and PR clients about his new job.

However, soon after the HR director said she would make flight arrangements for Sidney to come to their city to look for housing, Sidney realized that he wouldn't have time to finish one pending project before his employment start date a few weeks away. So what should he do?

# What Should Sidney Do?

Here are some possibilities. In Sidney's place, what would you do and why? What do you think the outcomes of these different options would be?

 Turn down the contract in the first place, since you aren't being offered enough and are certain to be resentful.

 Quietly do the project on your own time and not mention it, since it was just a small project, no big deal.

 Ask a lawyer to contact the company president for you, rather than sending an e-mail, to support your claim that you already had a contract for the job.

 Ask for an extra week to arrange your affairs before relocating to do the job, and complete the project during that extra week.

 Be relieved you didn't get the job and look for another, since you otherwise would be working for an unreasonable company in an unfamiliar place.

 Other?

Unfortunately, Sidney did the one thing he probably shouldn't—he pushed an already tense negotiation just a little too far. He sent the HR director another e-mail pointing out that he would be losing about $5000 in income for this already agreed upon project, and he said he had forgotten to include this provision in an exception clause for in-progress noncompetitive work. So, now, he asked, could he have permission to complete the project on his own time, or could he be put on the payroll a week early, while he was moving, to defray that lost income?

In his view, this was just a request, not a demand or a continuation of the earlier negotiations.

But to the company, his request was like asking for that extra nibble to get a little bit more. The result was that the HR director not only turned down his request in an e-mail but withdrew the company's offer of employment. Then, making matters worse, Sidney e-mailed the HR director asking to talk to the company president, stating that he already had a contract for employment and he couldn't be fired for cause for at least six months, to which the HR director said the president didn't want to talk to him.

In Sidney's mind, the company was being totally unfair, and had caused him lost work, time, and money, plus the embarrassment of having to explain why things didn't work out to his references and friends and associates he had told about his new job. So now he was wondering if he should bring in a lawyer. In his view, he had made a reasonable request to which the company could have easily said no—but instead had unreasonably pulled the job offer.

But was the company being unreasonable? From the company's point of view, it could easily seem like Sidney was asking for one more special exception to get more money after an already tense negotiation. So Sidney had pushed too far, without realizing that his final push was like the proverbial straw on the camel's back that sent his job hopes off a cliff.

Instead, what Sidney probably should have done was to complete the pending project before he left, give up the expected income if he couldn't finish the project since he was taking a new job, or quietly finish up the project if he could without asking for any more from the company or even alluding to the contract. After all, if he could finish the project on his own time without interfering with his new job, probably no one would know or care—and he could always explain, if necessary, later on that the project took longer than expected and he had a commitment to finish it. In short, backing off with a little diplomacy might have gone a long way to both keeping his job and his previous job commitment.

Likewise, if you're in a negotiation that's gone on for awhile and might be getting tense, pay attention to the cues you are getting from the other party. Are they starting to get tense and testy? Are they resisting your requests? Sometimes the strategy of being a hard bargainer and getting everything you can is exactly what you should not do. Sure, there are times to press forward, especially when you feel your skills and abilities are very much in demand. But once you sense that your requests seem to be triggering resistance or reluctance, it's better to back away—or the other party may back away first, and there goes your job or the deal.

# Today's Take-Aways:

 If you can't get everything you want, sometimes it may be better to take what you can get—without asking for more.

 Being a hard bargainer can turn into being a bad bargainer when asking for more becomes asking for too much.

 Watch out that a little nibble doesn't turn out to be the last bite that blows the deal.

 Thoroughly think through all your requests before you make them, so you don't find yourself wanting to ask for more later.

 Ask for everything you reasonably want in the beginning, since you can always pull back some of your requests later—as long as you don't ask for TOO much to kill the deal in the first place.

 Just like medicine, it goes down more easily when you take it in one gulp. When you ask for more later, it's like making someone have to take some more spoonfuls of medicine after she has put away the spoon and thinks she doesn't have to take anymore.

# 29

# What *to* Do When Everything Seems *to* Be Going Wrong

**H**ave you had those days when everything seems to be going wrong? It's like having the Midas touch in reverse—instead of things turning to gold, you touch them and they turn to lead. Such experiences not only leave us feeling upset and frustrated, they also make us start reflecting: Why is this happening? What am I doing wrong? Who could be doing this to me? And so on. The process is a little like what we as a nation are now going through as so many things are going wrong in our national life—from dot.com crashes to the continuing economic doldrums to the increasing instability on the international scene. Apart from the various military and security measures our country is taking recent events have triggered a time of deep national reflection.

What do you do when a series of reverses happens at work or in your life generally—or both? For instance, Sharon, a business consultant, had a series of problems on a day that started out bad and then got much worse. It started with an office computer system upgrade that took longer than expected followed by a call from a client who said his computer crashed, so he needed her to send the report again right away. But she needed to get her own computer working again before she could do that. Unfortunately, after waiting all day to use the computer, it still wasn't done and she had to tell the computer tech to come in the next day as well as call her client to explain the delay.

More problems developed when she rushed to the first day of her evening business class. Unfortunately, since she left later than planned, she encountered an accident on the bridge, which delayed her for about 20 minutes. She had to drive around the campus parking lot for several minutes to find one of the few remaining spots. Finally, she arrived at her first class late and famished, since she was in such a rush that she had skipped dinner.

Then, even more problems. When she returned from the break with some snacks and moved her chair, so she could hear the professor, her orange juice bottle fell, sending juice all over the floor. Of course this made her late joining the breakout groups for a teamwork exercise, as she stopped to mop up the floor. A few hours later, when she got back to her car, she discovered she had left the lights on in her rush to class, so the car wouldn't start. When she went to the office of the campus police for help, the officer at the desk said he couldn't leave the office to jump start her car since he was the only one on duty, and so he sent her to the auto body shop on campus. Though the mechanic gave her jumper cables with a battery box to start the car and instructions on what to do, once she started it, she was so tired and it was now so late and dark that she drove around the campus to return the cables, rather than walking back to the shop and then back to her car. Unfortunately, as she tried to find her way off campus by driving along the wide pedestrian walkways on the campus and on to the street, another campus cop saw her and stopped her, though he ultimately took pity on her, after she described her terrible day. So after a stern lecture about driving across the campus plaza, he sent her on her way. Yes, it was that kind of day, and everything had gone so wrong that it made Sharon wonder why. What had she possibly done that might have led to such havoc? Was there anything she should have done differently? Why did it all happen? Was there anything she could or should do now?

# What Should Sharon Do?

Here are some possibilities. In Sharon's place, what would you do and why? What do you think the outcomes of these different options would be?

 Take some time to meditate to relax and get more centered, so you do everything you are already doing—but only better and with less stress.

 Take a short weekend vacation to feel renewed and recharged— then the problem should go away.

 Take some time to reflect on what went wrong and why, so you can correct it.

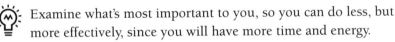 Turn to others for more help, so you can turn over some of your extra responsibilities to them.

 Examine what's most important to you, so you can do less, but more effectively, since you will have more time and energy.

 Other?

Sharon's experience led her to spend some time thinking about what she had been doing, and wondering what she should change. As a result of this self-examination, she came to realize that she was over-committed. She was doing too much, so she was continually rushing to get from one assignment to another, with the result that the slightest glitch could throw off her whole system, as it had that day. Thus, a good first step was dropping her business class. Then, she reflected on everything she was doing, so she could prioritize what was most important and do the first things first. It was like she used the day of disasters as a wake-up call and then started to pay attention to what she needed to do now.

What if everything seems suddenly to go wrong for you? How do you break the cycle and stop the process? Or how can you learn from what happened for the future?

A good first step is to take some quiet time to reflect on what has happened to learn why and consider what you might learn from the experience. When you do reflect, think back to when the chain of negative events started and examine what might have triggered them, much as Sharon looked back and realized she was doing too much, which made it difficult for her to complete everything, made her late, and set the other events in motion.

Then, once you have identified the causes or triggering event, you can take steps to counteract that cause. For example, if you are doing too much, do less. If you have a job or boss that is putting you under too much pressure, think about how you might change the present situation to reduce the pressure. Or perhaps consider if you need to do something so you won't react this way in the future, such as by taking more quiet time to relax each day or signing up for a yoga or karate class to experience a renewed sense of relief. Still another possibility might be turning to others you feel you can trust for help, such as asking for more assistance on a project or adding someone else with more expertise to a team.

In short, when things go wrong, take time to reflect on what has happened and why. Then, think about ways to correct the problem and learn from the experience, so you move on, better prepared for the future.

# Today's Take-Aways:

 Is everything suddenly going wrong? Ask yourself why.

 When everything starts going wrong, start thinking about what you can do to make it go right.

 Look on a series of bad experiences as a time to reflect and make changes, based on your insights about what these experiences are telling you.

# 30

# When *to* Keep Your Cards *to* Yourself

T he problem of inflated and fraudulent resumes is widely discussed today. According to estimates reported in the media, about a third of all resumes have false information and a third have exaggerations that misrepresent the truth. Sure, these deceptions may get you the job, and many people have gone on to great things once they are in the company and show their work. A prime example is the story of David Geffen, now one of the most powerful figures in Hollywood, who got his start in the William Morris mailroom with a false resume.

But increasingly in today's info-age, these lies are exposed and people lose jobs, from high-profile coaches and historians to people in every-day jobs. Even U.C. Berkeley's business school cracked down with back-ground checks on MBA candidates; they found that five of them had listed jobs they hadn't had, and dropped them from their roster of ac-cepted students. So given the ease of background searching and widely circulated information on the Internet, don't think you can hide.

Still, there may be times when you don't have to say anything and shouldn't. While you have to reveal key information—like the dates of previous jobs and education, you don't necessarily have to write down such information and there are times when you shouldn't. After all, there's no reason to unnecessarily raise the red flags yourself—or worse, wave them to say "Look at me." In other words, there are times to keep your cards to yourself and reveal them only if asked. But then, if you don't show them, no one may ask.

That's what almost happened to Joyce, a woman in her 50s who had returned to the workplace and was seeking a job as a counselor in a social welfare agency. She had gone back to school and had just graduated with an MA. in the field, after completing a paid internship at an agency in a larger city. This would be her first real paid job in the field.

But Joyce wasn't sure what to say about some problems she had encountered along the way. Should she put them in her covering letter, in her resume, or mention them in her interview? When she called me, she had already drafted a letter about what happened, along with an explanation. The problem? During her internship, she had worked with a particularly difficult supervisor who had required the employees to work extra overtime hours to handle an excess case load at a time when the city's social services' budget had been cut. But she also asked the employees not to put in for overtime. Grudgingly, the employees went along with the arrangement, but they often griped about it among themselves.

Joyce ran into problems when she went public with these complaints. Without mentioning any names, she told her supervisor that she and many other employees didn't think the extra hours without extra pay were fair. Instead, she stated, they should either be paid, not asked to work extra hours, or the agency should get more money from the city to compensate them for the overtime. Her supervisor was furious both by the particular demand and the challenge to her own power. The result was a big blowout argument in her supervisor's office, where her supervisor offered nothing but an ultimatum: "If anyone doesn't like this, they can leave." And after that, Joyce felt continually on the hot seat at work and experienced a very difficult last month of her internship. She even had to take several days off because of stress.

Now she was thinking of noting the incident in her job application letters. She proposed giving her side of the story and explaining that she was quite happy to work extra hours, if paid to do so. She also was considering including an explanation about her age, thinking that might be issue for a new supervisor who was 20 years younger than she. For instance, she thought she might mention that it sometimes took her a little longer to learn new information, but she could compensate for that by writing things down. Why say all this? Because Joyce was concerned the issues and questions might come up anyway; this way she could tell her side with her own explanation first. But was this the best approach for Joyce to take in seeking a new job?

# What Should Joyce Do?

Here are some possibilities. In Joyce's place, what would you do and why? What do you think the outcomes of these different options would be?

 Provide a good explanation for the problems that came up on her previous job; a potential employer will appreciate her forthrightness and candor.

 Describe how skilled she is at writing things down to compensate for her difficulty in learning new information; an employer will like someone who is commited to detail and accuracy.

 Leave the information about her problems on her internship off her resume and letter, since she completed the internship to graduate, and the issue will probably not come up.

 Say nothing about her problems with learning new information and compensating for it by writing things down, since employers are not supposed to ask about disabilities.

 Be ready to answer any questions about her weaknesses, should they come up, but otherwise, not volunteer any information.

 Other?

Fortunately, Joyce hadn't yet sent the letter, because, as I told her, you don't have to put everything down. Yes, you have to be truthful. But you don't have to wear your weaknesses on your sleeve. For example, why detail the problem with a supervisor in an internship unless the subject should come up? Very possibly it might not. After all,

Joyce had already gotten credit for the program towards her degree, so she could truthfully say she had successfully completed the internship and she wasn't using that supervisor as a reference since the program was over. Certainly, a reasonable explanation might deflect any further concern about not having the reference, and even if the former supervisor was called, former employers don't bring up past problems with former employees on their own. Given current privacy laws protecting employees, usually all an employer is likely to say is that a person worked there during a certain period of time. If necessary, Joyce could always respond to a question with an explanation of what happened. But there was no need to raise and wave around the red flag herself.

Likewise, since age information isn't required on resumes and employers aren't supposed to ask about it, there was no reason to bring up her age concerns. If Joyce already had a way to compensate for her difficulty in learning and remembering the information needed to do the job by writing it down, why bring that up either? If she could do the job, however she did it, that was what mattered, so there was no need to advertise her weaknesses. In short, she should, as they say, put her best foot forward, and not try to show off all the worn shoes in her closet.

Everyone has some weaknesses, and it's usually good to acknowledge them if they become relevant and try to improve on them or work around them. But otherwise, in a job or in whatever else you do, it's best to build on and show off your strengths. That way you appear confident, in charge, and show you can do the job. You don't want to explain all of the ways you can't or might not be able to do the work, for then you are very likely not going to be able to show all the ways you can do it.

Joyce did rewrite her letter. She left off the references to weaknesses and emphasized her own strengths that would make her especially qualified, such as her sensitivity and compassion for others and her concern for details and accuracy. Then, in her interview, she stressed her strengths, too. The reference to any conflicts with her former supervisor never came up, and eventually she got the job.

Likewise, should you be seeking a job or a promotion, do think about any weaknesses that might affect your performance and how to compensate for them. Be prepared to address them if asked, such as in response to the common interview question: "What is your greatest weakness?" But otherwise, don't dwell on your weak points, highlight them, or bring them up, unless you think the problem is almost certain to come up because it's part of your formal record that'll be revealed in an ordinary background check. For instance, while actual convictions may turn up in an ordinary background check, arrests may not, and private personnel records in a company generally stay just that—private, except under special circumstances, such as if you waive confidentiality and the company is willing to release those records. Thus, given such privacy protections, focus on your strengths and how you can contribute to an employer's success. That way you show confidence and the conviction you can do the job; you don't reveal your concerns that maybe you can't. Just like a card player, you don't want to let others know you are holding a hand of low cards, if you plan to stay in the game. Rather, you want to conceal those low cards, particularly if you have a chance to draw again and get a better hand.

# Today's Take-Aways:

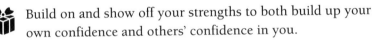

 Build on and show off your strengths to both build up your own confidence and others' confidence in you.

 Don't advertise weaknesses unless you can turn them into strengths —such as trying harder like Avis, because you're number 2.

 Don't worry that a person on a previous job will raise a conflict he had with you. Most likely he won't raise the issue, since he wants to keep these past problems private as much as you do.

 If your weaknesses aren't going to interfere with your doing the job, there's no need to bring them up.

 To get a job, show how you can do it; don't offer up reasons why maybe you can't.

Think of your weaknesses like your underwear; there's no need to show them off unless you have a good reason to take off your suit or dress.

# 31
## Watch Out *for* Warning Signs

S ometimes there are early signs that things aren't going to work out, if only you recognize them or take them seriously. If you see them soon enough, you might use them as a sign it's now time to get out or make changes, if you can. Or at least use them to feel better about whatever happened, so you don't get caught up blaming yourself or others when something at work doesn't work out.

Think of these signs as warnings. Take note of them, if only to put them on a shelf in your mind as a signal to pay special attention that there may be problems ahead. If there are, you are forewarned, though you may not be able to do anything about them at the time. But afterward, you might use these signs to help better understand what went wrong, notice organizational problems, or show why you don't want to take a particular job or work with a particular group.

That's what happened to Alan when he went to an introductory training session for a new job. Everything seemed so perfect. He was changing careers, and he was enthusiastic about joining a regional sales team for a company that sold management training programs around the United States. After training, his job would be to set up sales presentations at companies in his area to introduce the company's new product line, which featured a series of management training modules. Then, after each presentation, he was to send back meeting reports describing what happened. He was especially enthused because the company's project director had selected and hired him by only looking at his resume and at some sales reports and programs he had created as an MBA student. So he felt flattered by their seemingly high level of trust to hire him without even a telephone interview. Though he didn't know much about the company's programs or sales approach, just a brief description of the major components, he felt it was reasonable not to get this information, given the company's concern with confidentiality and secrecy. Thus, he thought it made sense that he would learn the details at the sales training, and since the company had hired him so quickly, well, that must mean the chemistry was just right. Or was it? In effect, the company management had created the conditions for future failure, without recognizing it themselves, and then blaming Alan for this failure when it occurred. But Alan just didn't see the early signs portending workplace doom.

The first sign of problems ahead, though Alan didn't think anything of it at the time, was when he helpfully found the flight times offered by different airlines and suggested a preferred flight. But Danny, the project director, sent him a confirmation for another flight that left about the same time, though it arrived slightly later at night and had a shorter connection time in the hub airport. At once Alan asked about changing it, wondering whether the 35-minute connection time would be long enough to make the connecting flight. But Danny quickly said no, sending an e-mail to say: "The other flight costs $500 more, so is it okay to keep that flight?" Of course, Alan said yes, feeling that if he objected, it would mean he wouldn't get the job.

When it came time to take his flight, however, there was an unexpected delay, since the flight crew discovered at boarding time that they were missing one crew member, and by the time a replacement got to the airport, the flight left 25 minutes late. As a result, Alan ended up spending the night at the connecting city, with the airline footing the bill. "No, it's not your fault," Danny assured him, even offering to pay for the room if the airline did not. "Just come as soon as you arrive," which is what Alan did.

Unfortunately, when he arrived about two and a half hours late, the training was already underway, and the newly recruited sales management team was gathered around a demonstration of how to present the program at each company. Though Alan had expected an introduction to the group or a short explanation to bring him up to speed, everyone was concentrating intently, so he simply called out a "Hello," which most ignored, and he went over to join the group. As he did, he felt fairly disconnected and alien, not sure what was going on.

Then, though he had no introduction to the sales technique just demonstrated, he was supposed to team up with a partner to role play the demo himself. He felt relieved when his partner Sandra suggested that she start off doing the presentation, after which they could alternate doing the different segments. But even after observing her initial presentation role play he still felt unsure of what to do.

Still, Alan thought Danny might explain more about the training during the lunch break, as Danny had said he would during their airport conversation. But Danny was busy setting up for the afternoon equipment demonstration, and told him: "You can read up on the details in the training folder," flipping quickly through a folder to show him that everything they had gone over in the morning session was right there. "Well, it would still help to know who's in the group," Alan said, and quickly Danny reeled off a list of names and cities, before running off to prepare the demo.

After lunch, as Danny described the equipment they would use to put on their presentation—a mix of cameras, projectors, and tape recorders—and described the lengthy sales pitch in more detail, Alan began to review the numbers in his head and project what his likely earnings might be. The more Danny spoke, the more hours Alan realized would be involved—from recruiting companies to participate in the program to putting on the presentation and writing up detailed sales reports so the company could refine the program. And then any payment would depend on any sales. But would there be any and how many? Alan began to wonder if the project was even feasible and cost effective. Yet here he was in the company's plush corporate headquarters for the training, where everyone else, much more experienced than he, seemed to believe in the project's great potential, which was one reason it was so hush-hush.

Still, despite these growing reservations, Alan pushed aside his concerns and focused on paying attention to the equipment demonstration.

But his many unanswered questions about the program, the prospects for recruiting participating companies, and questions about how to work the equipment, send in reports, and what to do if the equipment didn't work nagged at him. So from time to time, he asked them, and generally Danny gave helpful answers, though occasionally Danny pointed out that something had already been covered or would be. Danny also responded sharply a few times when Alan wondered why something was being done a certain way, thinking that there might be a simpler, easier, and faster way. "That's not negotiable," he said abruptly, with obvious annoyance. So Alan didn't press that point, but a few minutes later, he had other questions, as did other new members of the sales team, though not as many.

Then, suddenly, when Alan least expected it, during a coffee break, Danny asked him to get his things and come with him. Moments later, Danny told him firmly and brusquely: "This isn't open to any discussion or negotiation. I don't think you can succeed in the sales management program. You don't have the skills to do so." For a moment, Alan became defensive, wondering what he had done wrong. "Was it because I came late?," he asked. "Was it because I asked too many questions?" "Can you tell me what I need to do to fix whatever's wrong?" But Danny didn't want to explain, telling him only: "The decision is final and not negotiable. These things sometimes don't work out, and you don't know until you have a chance to meet each other personally."

So that was it. Over. Danny escorted Alan to get his bag and then out of the building to get a cab, so he could make an early flight at the airport. Oddly, however, instead of feeling upset or disappointed as one usually does in getting fired, Alan felt strangely relieved and free. He didn't have to take the job he realized he didn't want but that he wouldn't have backed out of himself, because he felt he had made a commitment, and because the company had paid for his training. But now that Danny had said no, he felt he was off the hook. The only thing he regretted was not knowing or acting sooner to turn down the project; then he wouldn't have had to spend three days flying back and forth on what turned out to be a useless trip. "Just think of all the other things I could have done instead," Alan thought to himself as the plane took off, though he was relieved he didn't have to take the job.

# What Should Alan Have Done?

Here are some possibilities. In Alan's place, what would you have done and why? What do you think the outcomes of these different options would be?

 Learn more about the sales program before taking the trip for the training; if the project director can't tell you more, don't go.

 Ask to take the flight with a longer connection time, and turn down the job if the project director won't make the change. That's a sign the employer is likely to take advantage of employees and doesn't think through the likely consequences of his or her actions.

 Cancel the trip once the flight is delayed, because it's likely you won't be able to make the connections—or even if you do, consider the delay a warning sign that maybe you shouldn't take the job.

 Ask for introductions and an update after arriving late, because you can't properly do a role play when you don't know your role.

 Tell Danny that he is requiring more of the sales management people than expected, and therefore you don't want the job.

 Other?

As Alan's story illustrates, at times signs all along the way indicate that things are wrong, such as when someone else has created a difficult, even unworkable situation, but you aren't aware of these problems at the outset. For example, here Danny and his team had set up a situation where Alan was bound to fail, though they attributed it to

Alan's lack of skills for the job. One problem was that in trying to save money for the flight they created a situation in which it was likely that Alan might miss the connecting flight if there was the slightest delay, which there was—a common occurrence in airline travel today. Second, the project director didn't take the time to welcome Alan, introduce him to others, and fill him in so he would know what was going on. Instead, he was thrown into a setting where he wasn't prepared with the necessary skills for the follow-up role play. Another problem is that because of the company's concern with secrecy and confidentiality, the project director hadn't fully filled in Alan about the expectations and time commitment involved in the job. And he didn't recognize that Alan's many questions were due to his effort to get informed, because the project director hadn't done his job, not because Alan wasn't competent to do his. Alan walked into a situation already set up for failure, and he was justified in feeling relieved to be out of it; though ironically, Danny both set and sprung the trap.

Yet, did Alan have to get caught in the trap in the first place? Perhaps he might have avoided it had he seen some of the early warning signs along the way, and considered some of the problems that might occur. For instance, when Danny first proposed the flight plan with the short connection time, maybe Alan might have urged the more expensive flight because of the potential connection problems, even if this meant not getting the job. Then, when Alan learned the flight was going to be delayed, maybe he could have realized the likelihood of the missed connection and seen that as a sign not to take the flight and to turn down the job. Or perhaps even earlier he might have asked for more information and asked more questions about what was expected, rather than feeling flattered he was hired so quickly. For with this extra information, he might have realized the extensive time required to set up and give sales presentations that might be hard to arrange, resulting in low commissions or even no commissions—and then he might not have signed on for the training in the first place.

In short, as they say, "Look before you leap," and that means looking for signs that maybe you shouldn't leap at all. Or if you do, once you think about the signs you missed along the way, you blame yourself or feel regret, because you can't work in an unworkable situation that isn't right for you. Instead, view whatever happened as a learning experience letting you know that you have to pay closer attention to signs of problems ahead in the future. Then you will be less likely to take an ill-advised future leap. You will be less likely to step off the cliff, because you will see the drop-off ahead.

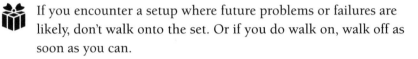

# Today's Take-Aways:

 If you encounter a setup where future problems or failures are likely, don't walk onto the set. Or if you do walk on, walk off as soon as you can.

 To see the warning signs of future difficulties, watch for them on the road ahead—just like you do when you look for signs when driving.

 It's easy to miss the signs of problems if you're moving ahead too fast. So slow down and take more time to look around to make sure of a clear path ahead.

 Even experts may not see the signs that they have created a setup for failure; so look for the signs yourself.

The more signs of problems you see, the more it's time to sign off.

Signs are like smoke signals that indicate where there's smoke there's fire and the possibility of a conflagration—or a whole lot of trouble—ahead.

# 32
# Don't Resign Yourself— *Redesign* Yourself

I n today's climate of dot.com and high-tech layoffs, many people are running scared. People are afraid that the next job axe may fall on them; that the next business cutback will chop off their clients. Still other changes and readjustments in the workplace are due to more and more cross-cultural diversity across and within departments. Thus, this fast pace of change may leave you breathless and hoping for more stability, and your hopes to redesign your current job around your current skills may not work either.

For some people, such developments are demoralizing. They see the writing on the wall that looks like "Up and out!" But you don't have to *resign* yourself to becoming one more statistic in the turbulent new economy. Instead, think how you can *redesign* yourself to create a new improved future for yourself. Like the chameleon, be ready to change your colors as the environment shifts around you.

I received several e-mails in response to my column on workplace issues from readers who were facing this adjustment to change problem. One woman—let's call her Jackie—wrote to me telling me she started a new job about two months earlier as a counselor in a social service agency dealing primarily with Hispanic families. While she had great credentials as a counselor from previous agencies she had worked for and a certificate in her field, her problem was that she didn't speak

Spanish, and she had replaced a counselor who spoke both Spanish and English. Even her supervisor spoke the two languages. At one time, the agency had mostly English-speaking clients, but the community had changed because of increased immigration.

So why had the agency hired Jackie in the first place? The supervisor was impressed by Jackie's past work history and hadn't thought there would be any language barrier. After all, the new immigrants were supposed to learn English. But apparently they didn't learn it fast enough in order to communicate with Jackie, because many were older immigrants and it took more time for them to learn a new language than it would children or teenagers. And so Jackie wrote me describing how hard it was for her to learn her new job in what was essentially a foreign culture. Because of these difficulties, she was becoming increasingly upset and emotional on the job. She felt even worse when she saw her supervisor communicating with other counselors in Spanish. Now she was concerned about an upcoming meeting with her supervisor, since she was in a six-month probation program. Did this mean the end of her job, and what should she do?

# What Should Jackie Do?

Here are some possibilities. In Jackie's place, what would you do and why? What do you think the outcomes of these different options would be?

 Ask her employer to supply a translator, since it's not her responsibility to learn a new language; the immigrants are supposed to learn English.

 Find another job where the clients do speak English.

 Ask her supervisor to give her time off and cover the costs of any training if she needs to learn Spanish, since this is extra work, not part of her original work agreement.

Speak to an employment attorney about preserving her rights to keep her job or gain compensation, if she is unfairly terminated because she shouldn't be required to learn Spanish.

 Other?

**P**robably the first step, should she want to stay on the job, is obvious—learn Spanish to communicate better not only with the clients but also with the other staffers. She also needed to recognize that this wasn't a job she could easily redesign, say by dividing up her tasks with others, since she had to work directly with the Spanish-speaking clients. She couldn't effectively counsel them if she needed a translator, because this would undercut the rapport she needed to communicate with them, as well as requiring the additional expense of a translator in an agency that already had a limited budget. Thus, she needed to repackage, re-create, re-mobilize, and re-motivate herself to do the job effectively. (Yes—all the "re" words—meaning do it differently and better). Ideally, she might be able to persuade her current employee to cover the costs of the training and give her time off to attend. But realistically, in a cost-strapped social service agency, that might not be possible, and the added language ability might help her in the future in any other agency in the area given the change of demographics. So it might well be worth it to simply take some classes in the evening, and costs might be minimal through a local community college evening program. In short, she should be the one to change and adapt, given the changing conditions needed to do her job effectively.

But beyond planning such a basic personal revamping, when you re-design yourself, let others know, so they see you growing and changing and want to help. As I wrote back to Jackie in an e-mail: "Perhaps look into taking some Spanish classes or ask your supervisor about your plans to show you want to learn."

In addition, find out more specifically what you need to learn. As I continued on in my message: "Perhaps talk to your supervisor or someone else you feel is most supportive of you to find out what you need to do the job well. If you are on a probation period and you want to stay, find out what you need to do to perform the job effectively, show that you really want to do this, and seek their help to put these efforts into action. This way you show your motivation to do a good job and learn, and that might help your supervisor want to continue to support you and help you succeed."

If you are facing such a situation in which you need new skills of any sort, you must learn what additional skills you need to learn, seek help from mentors, coaches, teachers, peers, or others who might help you learn, and then start learning. The sooner you take action, the better— because this way, you don't have to resign yourself to losing out or falling behind—or get resigned (ie: terminated or laid off by someone else). Instead, with a personal redesign, you're back in the game, like a whole new package. Just like companies refresh their packages to reappeal to consumers when they are losing market share, refresh and repackage yourself to increase your own appeal. Find a way to redesign a NEW IMPROVED YOU!

# Today's Take-Aways:

 Once you *redesign* yourself, you don't have to *resign* yourself.

 The change from "resign" to "redesign" is just two letters, but there's a world of difference when you add them—like adding spice to the soup.

 Think of yourself as your own "redesign director"—you just need to bring together the right skills and right team to make your redesign work.

# 33

# Be *a* Problem Solver—Theirs, Not Yours

**K**eeping up in today's competitive and fast changing work environment can be a problem, especially when you have to keep learning new skills and strategies and fear your job or business could be the next to go. Some people even start thinking grievance or lawsuit when they find that the promises made to them when they are first hired by a struggling or downsizing company have not been kept. Or they feel they are unfairly marked for an early termination or retirement, perhaps because they are earning more, are older, or have been more recently hired. Whatever the reason for the problem, a good way to think about it—and help you keep your job or business—is to see the situation not as *your* problem, but as *their* problem. Then, think about how you can help them solve it. After all, if you turn yourself into the answer to their problems, you may find the answer to your own.

I received an e-mail from a man—let's call him Henry—who was recently let go from a big company he had worked at for over 15 years. He had been a model and enthusiastic sales employee, even driving for about two hours a day to get to work—one hour there, one hour back— and he had built up a loyal customer base throughout his West Coast sales territory. But then, the corporation, which was based on the East Coast, hit by reduced sales and the need to downsize, decided to make some changes in its operations and brought in a new Regional Manager,

Tony, who had the right to hire and fire any employees. In the ensuing shakeup, the Regional Manager brought in a new younger team, and Henry, now in his early 50s, was out. Worse, Henry was especially disturbed by some of the insulting things Tony said to him about his personal style. Tony had complained that he was disorganized and that his personality rubbed him the wrong way, even though Tony couldn't fault Henry's good sales record.

The firing rankled, especially since Henry found himself stuck with temporary low pay assignments as he scrambled to find work at other companies over the next few years. Then, a ray of hope. Henry's old company brought in a new Regional Manager who was a long-term friend of Henry's and hoped to rehire Henry, but the home office nixed the rehire. After all, if Henry had once been let go, why hire him again?

# What Should Henry Do?

Here are some possibilities. In Henry's place, what would you do and why? What do you think the outcomes of these different options would be?

 Write to the home office and explain the reasons you should be hired again, such as knowing the company and the territory very well.

 Contact an employment lawyer to negotiate for getting your job back or face an age discrimination suit.

 Learn more about the company and its problems and suggest some solutions that you can provide, if you are back on the job.

 Offer to get some additional training, even if you have to foot the bill yourself, to show how deeply motivated you are.

 Offer to work for less or agree to a trial probationary period to show what you can do.

 Other?

W hat should Henry do? Ideally, he wanted his old job back, but he was also wondering if he had the basis of a lawsuit because of age discrimination or the insulting way he had been fired. My advice to Henry—or to anyone in a similar situation—is to forget the lawsuit. Commonly they take years and extensive time and effort to pursue, even if you do meet all the requirements to be able to pursue a case, and in the meantime your life may go on hold. The company you are suing is unlikely to hire you back while the suit is ongoing and it could be a very uncomfortable working environment even if you are, since everyone will know about the suit. And if you don't work there, other companies in your field will be even less likely to hire you.

So don't use a club if you want to get rehired, since you're likely to get clubbed back in return, and it could be a long time, if ever, for you to get a job back that way. Also, if you want another job in that industry, the memory of a lawsuit, whether you win or lose, can be like a memo reminding others not to hire you either for fear you might later sue them. Certainly, there are times when you don't want to let your rights be trampled, say when the discrimination against you is so clear and so outrageous and your case is one that gains widespread support from others for your unfair treatment. But in general, look on lawsuits as a last resort—and avoid them if at all possible. Find other win–win ways to try to work out your differences; look for compromises and collaborations rather than confrontations when you aren't in a power position to readily get your own way.

Thus, as I e-mailed Henry, his best shot at getting his job back would be to become a kind of problem solver for the company he wanted to work for. In other words, help them solve their problem as the route to solving his own. For instance, I suggested he might find out a little more about the corporation's current situation and what kind of workers they were looking for after a period of downsizing and reorganization. Ask probing questions to understand better just what's going on. Then, he should look at how to sell himself to them based on what kind of benefits he could offer them, given their needs. "See what kinds of skills they need and ask if you need any new training to fit in with their current direction," I wrote. "Perhaps be prepared to compromise on salary if that is an issue in these downsizing times." The result was that Henry was invited to work with the company on the basis of looking for new business opportunities in expanded markets. While there was no guaranteed draw, there was a generous commission, giving him the opportunity to use his abilities to establish new accounts in new areas, helping both the company and himself.

In short, whatever the problem, the best approach is not to focus on past recriminations but on future solutions. For instance, see yourself as a problem solver and think about what your prospective or current employer's problems are and how you can help them solve them. Re-define the problem from *how can you get* a job or promotion to *how can you help* your company or employer do a better job of doing whatever they want to do. Then, you'll be part of that solution leading to the job or promotion. In effect, the way to sell yourself is not to sell you but the benefits you can offer a company. Sell yourself as a problem solver who can offer just what they need when they need it, and you'll solve your own problems by solving theirs.

# Today's Take-Aways:

 To solve a problem at work, try looking at it from a different perspective—theirs, not yours.

Turn your problems into opportunities by thinking of new ways to solve them with your employer's needs in mind.

 Look for the "probe" in "*prob*lems, and then probe for solutions to someone else's problems, not your own, to make yourself an essential part of the solution.

# 34

# Dealing *with the* Boss *from* Hell

Tyrants may eventually inspire revolts or the intervention of outside sympathetic third parties to overthrow them—as in the toppling of Saddam in Iraq. But the process doesn't often work that way in the workplace, when you have a tyrannical boss who calls the shots. He or she is fully in power—the owner of the company or in charge with the support of the top executives and board. Should you seek to foment workplace rebellion, you are likely to be quickly out of the company, unless you are able to muster the support of others who feel similarly mistreated. So besides leaving the job and seeking the best recommendation you can get as you go out the door, what do you do if, aside from the boss, you like the job or really need it? How do you handle your uncomfortable and hurt feelings?

That's what happened to May, when she landed her first job out of grad school doing research for a business consulting company that provided clients with research reports. She looked at the job as an ideal way to get the experience she needed to advance in the field. She also loved doing the work, which involved burrowing through company reports and Internet intelligence to come up with pithy analyses. She found the other researchers great to work with, and felt an instant warm camaraderie with them. Plus the company had a sterling reputation—it would be like graduating with a degree from Harvard when she was ready to take her next step up the career ladder.

But then there was her boss, Mildred, who acted like a tyrant of her workplace, in love with power. Mildred gave the orders, and if you didn't understand—well, that was your fault. You should have listened and learned the first time. If you didn't, you'd be subject to one of her rants. Meanwhile, the employees in the research department, mostly younger women new to the work world, quietly and submissively followed Mildred's orders. The feeling was you get along or get out.

But May was having an especially tough time of it, since she was used to working independently on research projects, where she would think through the best and most efficient way to do a job and get praised for her innovation and creativity. By contrast, Mildred allowed only her way; you follow the rules or else. Moreover, you better listen and understand what to do when she told you, or you would face a rant in her office, an angry memo, or a dressing down in front of the other employees—like facing the wrath of an angry deity.

Now, things seemed to be getting even worse, and May was feeling increasingly stressed and desperate. For example, one day Mildred asked her to attend an important conference, where May was supposed to take detailed notes and pictures and then use them for a conference report for a client. Mildred gave her a list of rules to follow, and concluded by saying: "Remember, your role is just to blend in, observe, and record. Don't talk to anyone who's working." "Certainly, will do," May agreed, and on the day of the conference, after saying a quick hello to Mildred to let her know she was there, May quietly spent the day carefully taking notes and photos as Mildred requested. She also got useful input from many participants who attended the event.

However, the next day, as she was writing up her report, Mildred called her to come into her office and began yelling at her. "What did I tell you about not talking to anyone?"

"But I didn't" May began. But before she could finish, Mildred was on the attack again. "Well, you came over to me while I was giving instructions to the moderators."

May tried to explain that she had just come over to say "Hello" to be polite and let Mildred know she was there, thinking it would be rude not to identify herself. But Mildred only used her explanation as fuel for further attack. "Then you didn't understand what I told you. I said don't TALK to anyone. If something isn't clear to you in the first place, you need to ask."

But how could May know to ask if something that had seemed so clear to her was meant so differently by her boss, who considered "not talking" to mean total silence and absolutely no interaction—not merely "no questions and no conversation," as May and her other co-workers interpreted these words. But with Mildred, there was no way to successfully dispute her interpretation, so May backed down. Even so, Mildred continued her rant, further berating May for other mistakes she made covering the conference, such as taking a photograph when all the presenters came together to pose for a photographer at the end of the conference. That was wrong because that was an official photograph, and May should have known not to take that. "It's in the list of rules I gave you," Mildred said firmly.

Afterwards, May was near tears when she returned to her office to write up her report. All she could think of was how unjust Mildred had been in her accusations and how unreasonable Mildred had been to not listen to her explanations or take any responsibility for the communications being unclear. Yet despite all the verbal abuse, May still wanted to hang onto her job, and she did her best to control her shaky emotions as she finished writing her report. What should May do to deal with her boss?

# What Should May Do?

Here are some possibilities. In May's place, what would you have done or do now and why? What do you think the outcomes of these different options would be?

 Forget the job and career advancement opportunities. You've got to get out and get out fast for your own sanity.

 Take Mildred's messages to heart, even if she is abrasive and hard to work with. Maybe you really do have communication problems, and you have to listen more carefully.

Don't take what Mildred has said personally. Just listen, acknowledge what she has said, and agree you will do better. Then, keep on working as best you can.

 Ask Mildred to have some personal time with her to express your feelings about how she has been unfairly berating you.

 Find a way to relax and release the tensions you have experienced after a brow-beating from Mildred; then try to focus on the work at hand.

 Talk to higher-ups in the company or speak to other employees who feel as you do, and try to organize a group protest to higher management.

 Other?

W hile there are many possible options to reasonably pursue, one of the most important considerations here is the importance of this job as a steppingstone for the future. If May is relatively new to the field, relatively powerless, truly likes the job though not the boss, and wants to use the job to move onto better things, probably it is best not to leave or rock the boat. Leaving would mean losing the valuable experience May is gaining doing research she loves. Confronting a boss who is an obsessive stickler for rules, judgmental of others, and thinks "My way is the only way" is probably not going to work well either, particularly since May is new to the job.

Normally, the boss should be the one to take responsibility if communications are unclear and should make sure the employees understand instructions and further clarify and explain them, when employees don't understand or don't know to ask for clarifications. But in this case Mildred is clearly not willing to do that. Moreover, a judgmental person who thinks he or she is always right is not going to be persuaded should an underling point out that he or she is wrong. Instead, this obsessive judge is likely to get still angrier. Then, too, contacting higher-ups or trying to organize others in the department is a highly risky move, especially for a newcomer. May could likely be ignored, soon be out of a job, or become the center of uproar in the office, none of these outcomes are very good prospects for someone just starting out with high hopes to continue in the field.

Rather it's probably best for May to learn to make the best of a difficult situation, such as by finding ways to relax and relieve stress and reminding herself not to take things personally. Looking for ways to work as independently as possible to reduce the number of encounters with Mildred might help, too, as would doing high-quality work—all very possible strategies given the nature of May's work doing research.

That's exactly what May did. She carefully read Mildred's memos; took careful notes when Mildred gave instructions; and then, as best she could, she sought to follow the procedures Mildred set forth to the letter, even when she felt there was a better, more efficient way to find information. But if Mildred asked her to check certain sources first or write up her notes in a certain way, that's exactly what she did. At the same time, she found ways to control her feelings when Mildred read her the latest riot act, such as using self-talk to tell herself: "Calm down, don't take it personally, just take it and relax," while Mildred ranted on and she verbally agreed with whatever Mildred said. Afterwards, when she did her research, she used more self-talk to refocus herself on the work, rather than her thoughts about Mildred's tirade. She also quietly shared her experiences with a few other employees who felt the same way, so they had a feeling of mutual support; they didn't have to share Mildred's verbal attacks alone. Also, from time to time, after Mildred berated her over the latest miscommunication or misunderstanding, she sent Mildred a memo in which she both apologized and explained why she had done what she understood she was directed to do. In this way, by sending a written memo, she could avoid confronting Mildred directly or suggesting that any Mildred did was wrong, while trying to explain what she did. The result was that May's "get along and get experience before you get out" strategy worked well, and she stayed on the job for several more months, gaining valuable experience, before she was ready to move on.

What if you are in a similar situation with a tyrannical boss? A good starting point is to assess your options. What's more important to you—

staying on the job for now or getting out? If you're leaving, go as gracefully as you can, so you don't burn up your chances for a good recommendation. But if you're going to stay, look for ways to get along better by doing it the way the tyrant boss wants even if this isn't the best way. Learn what the rules are and follow them as precisely as you can. Yes, you do become a "yes" man or woman. Yes, this may not be the most efficient, effective way to run a department or a company.

But if you focus on doing good work, while saying "yes," that's a key to survival. Much like in any tyrannical regime, it's the "yes" men who keep their heads. So as long as you aren't asked to do anything illegal or unethical and can do good quality work, think of what you are doing as doing "good" time, as they call it in prison. This way, you accumulate your time and your merits, so when the opportunity arises, you can use this "good" time to get out and gain success when you leave. You've worked hard and have acquired the skills and experience you need to help you in the future. So when you do get your freedom, you're good to go.

# Today's Take-Aways:

 If you really want to keep your job despite a tyrannical boss, find ways to go along to get along, so later you can better get out when the going is good.

 If you've got to get along in a difficult situation, find ways to relax and relieve stress, so you are better able to get along. In other words, if you have to stay on the path, clear out the rocks along the way to create a smoother place to walk.

 Just like real-world tyrants, tyrannical bosses are looking for people to say "yes." So learn to say "yes," "yes," and "yes." Think of saying "yes" as the way to survive and keep your head, as long as you have to work with this tyrant. Then learn what you can, so you can flee the regime on better terms when you have a good opportunity to move on.

# PART VI

# Putting It Together

# 35

## Mastering Your Survival Skills

As the stories in the previous chapters have illustrated, it not always easy to figure out what to do in a different situation—and there are many possible alternatives. Even if you choose what seems to be an optimal course of action at the time, you may not have all the facts or information you need; you may be hampered by faulty assumptions you can't check; you may have to choose between alternatives before you feel ready; you may be constrained by time and budget limits. Then, too, your personality and that of others you are dealing with affects what the best approach might be, as does the influence of your organizational culture, personal and organization priorities, and other factors.

The "What Should You Do?" questions in each chapter reflect this range of possibilities, and while some may be obviously wrong choices, others could be real options. Thus, while I have provided suggestions on what to do, what someone should have done, or why someone's actions were a mistake might vary in any given situation. Different people might have found a good alternative that worked well for them but might not work as well for someone else.

Thus, consider my suggestions to be more like well-reasoned, common-sense, creative, win–win, or other likely possibilities for success. But other reasonable alternatives might still exist that could result in success, too.

In short, there's no exact science in figuring out the best approach to promoting good relationships, solving problems, or resolving conflicts in the workplace. Humans, individually and even more in group relationships, are too complex, and the workplace setting with its mix of personalities, rules, regulations, customs, policies, politics, changing situations, and varied environmental influences, makes for even more complexity.

Still, it is possible to develop approaches, such as I have used in The *Survival Guide to Working with Humans,* to improve your chances of coming up with a good choice or solution. Then, you can apply these different approaches as appropriate to dealing with a particular situation.

Accordingly, this last chapter describes the range of approaches I use in figuring out what to do in different circumstances. A good way to think of these different approaches is to view these as having a repertoire of techniques you can draw on, much like a golfer might choose different clubs to make different types of shots on the green. By knowing how to use these techniques effectively, as well as when to use which approach or which combination of approaches, you will be better able to draw quickly on the appropriate technique or techniques as needed.

While these different techniques might merit a book themselves— in fact, I have written several books describing them: *Resolving Conflict; Work With Me: Resolving Everyday Conflict in Your Organization; Mind Power: Picture Your Way to Success in Business; The Empowered Mind: How to Harness the Creative Force Within You;* and *Making Ethical Choices, Resolving Ethical Dilemmas*—here I just briefly describe the major techniques I have used or recommend using in that situation. You can then use the approaches that feel the most comfortable for you or that seem the most suitable for a particular situation in your workplace environment.

While I have described these as separate techniques, in practice, as you work with these methods, they become second nature and can readily be combined. So rather than you having to think "I'm going to use this approach this time," the relevant techniques to apply start up automatically like mental computer programs that interact together to give you a suggested answer. As a result, when I think about how to deal with a specific situation, the possibilities or the alternative that seems the most optimal quickly come to mind. For me, they appear like images that play out on a series of monitors in a TV or film studio, though for others they may come up more in the form of words or dialogues in your mind or just a sense of knowing or feeling what to do. Typically, I see these images play out as if they are in fast-forward, so I can imagine different possible outcomes, as well as quickly consider costs and benefits, advantages and disadvantages, upsides and downsides, risks and returns—however you want to think of weighing the positives and negatives of a possible outcome.

Yet, while it may sound like this approach to thinking of alternative options and outcomes is a long process when broken down into components, in fact the process occurs almost instantaneously. It operates much like inputting a description of a problem or difficult situation into a computer, pressing a button, and seconds later, the screen shows a suggested solution. It may take some time initially to develop this mode of rapid processing to choose which techniques to use individually or in combination. But as you work with different methods, as in practicing any skill, at first you have to concentrate and think about what you are doing in a more logical, rational way. However, gradually, with practice, exercising the skill becomes integrated into your unconscious; it becomes so natural—you no longer have to think about it; you just do it.

Thus, as I describe different approaches I use, think of them as skills for processing information, problem-solving, and decision-making. As you become more familiar with them and use them regularly, they will become second nature. In fact, some may be approaches you might already use yourself, perhaps without thinking about them.

## A Toolbox of Techniques for Thinking About and Improving Relationships at Work

A few metaphors for thinking about these different techniques is to think of them as a set of tools in a toolbox, a collection of healing plants in a garden, or a selection of software for carry out different tasks. Whatever the metaphor, these are basically a repertoire of techniques you can draw on separately or together to help you better understand what's going on and what to do about it. The tools in this repertoire include:

### Visualizing Possible Options and Outcomes

Visualization or mental imaging is an extremely powerful way of looking at a situation. Essentially, you see it like a series of photos or a film or stage play occurring in your mind's eye. You get a clear picture of what is happening now and then visualize what might happen in the future, based on what actions you take now. As you do, you can either see the situation play out in one or more ways, based on the different actions you take, or you can skip ahead in your mind to the last frame and see the result of each approach.

You can also combine this visualization with other techniques, such as doing a cost–benefits or pro–con analysis to choose what you want to do. Such visualizing works well for problem-solving generally, as well as for thinking about relationships and how to improve them.

Generally, I go through the whole process very quickly in my head and quickly imagine what seems to be the best alternative under the circumstances. But some people, especially when first starting to use visualization, prefer to write down the different alternatives as they envision them or soon after concluding the process. Then, the take some time to do a more detailed cost–benefits or pro–con analysis, before deciding which alternative to choose, such as described in my books on using this method: *Mind Power: Picture Your Way to Success* and *The Empowered Mind: How to Harness the Creative Force Within You.* Alternatively, you can start by doing a more detailed analysis; then as you become more familiar with the process, let the alternatives and your choices play out in your head.

### Using Visualization for Goal Setting, Preparation, and Planning

Here visualization is used not so much to think of alternatives, but to imagine what you want for an outcome. Then, with this desired end clearly in mind, you think about what steps you need to take to get there—say to develop a better relationship with your boss or to plot out your next steps along a career path.

One way to use this approach is to visualize a linear outline of steps to take in your mind or perhaps see a single path to your goal with a series of stops along the way. Alternatively, you can't create an even more dramatic and dynamic mental visualization, such as seeing the goal you have set for yourself on a mountaintop with a series of places along the path where you can go for insights and information.

Whatever imagery you prefer to use, you can combine it with symbols, affirmations, self-talk, and reinforcements to help you feel more powerful and confident in making and implementing your choices. For instance, to have an effective real-time meeting with your boss to ask for a promotion or new project assignment, visualize and practice the meeting in your mind; make affirming statements about how you will get the project; and experience the symbol of fire or see a powerful animal giving you a surge of energy and power. Then, you bring the actual approach imagined in your visualization and the sense of power it gives you to the meeting you have in reality.

Since different styles of visualizing to set goals, prepare, and plan appeal to different people, it's best to find your own style that feels most comfortable for you.

## Doing What's Practical Through Weighing the Positives and Negatives

In making any decision or setting any goal and trying to achieve it, you also have to consider what's practical—essentially by doing a positive–negative, cost–benefit, or pro–con analysis. You can do such an analysis in a more organized, analytical way, such as taking listing the pros and cons for each of the alternative scenarios you choose, using weighted numbers to compare and contrast them. However, another method is to do a weighted comparison in a more holistic way, using a more intuitive, instant analysis process. In this case, the assessment of what's practical simply appears in your mind, as if you are letting your unconscious sort through the information and come up with the answer for you.

Such an instant intuitive analysis may seem difficult at first if you are new to visualizing. But this processing method can develop over time, and works well when combined with visualizing different possibilities. You start with imagining all that might be desirable. Then you add a consideration of what's most practical to the mix.

## Using the E-R-I Model for Resolving Conflicts

Another method I use for resolving conflicts is the "E-R-I" Model, in which the "E-R-I" stands for the Emotions, Reasons, and Intuition. This method is based on first getting the emotions out of the way—whether your own or someone else's. Then, use your reason to understand the reasons for the conflict by recognizing the different views, interest, personalities, and positions involved. In addition, use your reason to understand the different styles of resolving a conflict that you or the other parties to the conflict might use. These five styles are:

- *Confrontation,* where you exercise your power to seek what you want;

- *Collaboration,* where you and other parties to the conflict take time to consider the different issues and resolve them together;

- *Compromise,* where you each give a little;

- *Accommodation,* where you basically give in to what someone else wants because he or she has more power or the issue isn't that important to you;

- *Avoidance,* where you essentially don't deal with the conflict by leaving, not thinking about it, or delaying any action.

In the last step of the model, you use your intuition to brainstorm different alternatives and chose among them. It's an approach I have described at greater length in two of my books: *Resolving Conflict* and *Work With Me: Resolving Everyday Conflict in Your Organization.*

This approach also works well with visualization, in that you can visualize using different conflict resolution approaches and imagining different outcomes. Then, if you apply the cost–benefits approach, you can assess which of these outcomes might be best to use under the circumstances. Or you can let your intuition give you a quick answer of what feels like the best approach to adopt right now.

## Considering Differing Ethical Approaches to Resolve Ethical Issues

If a conflict involves ethical questions, I additionally draw on an Ethical Choices Model for understanding the ethical approaches of different people to help make choices that best fit with their own ethical values. This approach can also help to resolve any misunderstandings that occur when people have different ethical approaches.

A first step to using this ethical analysis is to understand the four major dimensions that shape each person's approach to ethics. These are whether a person is:

- *More or less practical or moral* in his or her values or philosophy;

- *More or less rational or intuitive* in his or her style;

- *More or less of a follower/conformist or an innovator/rule breaker* in his or her attitude toward rules;

- *More or less altruistic or self-interested* in his or her orientation to others and themselves.

This Ethical Choices Model creates a four-way matrix, much like the approach to personality typing used in the widely known Myers–Briggs Personality-Type Instrument, and it's described in more detail in *Making Ethical Choices, Resolving Ethical Dilemmas*. The advantage of understanding your own ethical approach and that of others you are interacting with is that you can better recognize different values, attitudes, styles, and orientations in different situations to help decide what to do.

For example, say you know someone is very concerned about doing what's right. You can appeal to them based on emphasizing ideas of fairness or justice. By contrast, if someone is more practically oriented, your appeal will be stronger if you emphasize what works and doesn't and how a proposed action will benefit that person or their organization.

### Other Major Considerations: Communications, Assumptions, Personalities, and Politics in the Workplace

Finally, a few issues come up repeatedly in causing misunderstandings, problems, and conflicts in the workplace; many times, addressing these issues will help to resolve other problems. For example, a communications breakdown often occurs because one person doesn't communicate something clearly or someone else misunderstands a message. Sometimes a key to improving a relationship or solving a problem is clarifying that communication or dealing with the fallout that results from the mis-understandings that occur when communications are unclear.

Wrong assumptions are also at the heart of many problems and con-flicts, because people don't have the facts, jump to conclusions based on making faulty assumptions, and act accordingly, even if those assump-tions are wrong. A key to reducing such problems is to check whether your assumptions are correct or to recognize that someone else is act-ing on faulty assumptions and correcting this error

Then, too, understanding personalities and special ways of dealing with particular personality types, including people viewed as "difficult people," can help to know what to do. For instance, if you are dealing with a control freak of a boss or colleague, you need to act to help them feel in control in order to defuse the anxieties they may feel in a partic-ular situation. By contrast, when you interact with someone who is very loose and relaxed, you can create better rapport by taking more time to slow down, engage in informal conversation to create a more personal bond, and then deal with the issue at hand.

Further, there are the realities of office politics. To learn what they are, you need to figure out the players and the terrain and rules by which they are operating, so you can better navigate through the political dy-namics in that office environment.

## Putting It All Together

When it comes to dealing with any specific situation, any and all of the above factors can come into play. Here I have presented a brief synop-sis of how these factors play a part, though each element could be a book in itself—from those I have written myself to the great many books by other authors.

To me, these techniques are like different tools to use in figuring out what to do when different issues, problems, or conflicts arise, such as described in this book. Obviously, the number of situations is infinite. The stories highlighted here are just some of the many situations that occur day to day in the workplace. In some cases, you may find parallels with incidents you have faced yourself; in other cases, even if the situations are different, the ways of resolving them are methods you might use in other contexts. Or these situations or methods of dealing with them might resonate for someone you know.

In any event, think of these stories much like modern-day workplace fairytales, legends, myths, and folk tales that are true and provide a moral or lesson like these traditional stories. Through these stories I have sought to highlight various principles for improving relationships, while using the methods described in this book to help figure out what is wrong and what needs to be done to resolve the problem or conflict. In future books, I'll be featuring other stories, and I invite you to send in your own stories, which I'll seek to resolve in a personal response to you, as well as use in future books.

So now, here's hoping you "work it right" to survive better in working with other humans! To see how well you're doing, take the "Work-Ability" (also called the "Work Survivability" quiz at the end of this book. See how well you score, based on how well you work it right and survive in the workplace.

# What Are the Major Techniques for Working It Right?

Here are the major techniques to use. How do you think you might use them individually and together and with what results? Can you think of other techniques you might use, too?

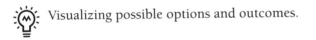 Visualizing possible options and outcomes.

 Using visualization for goal setting, preparation, and planning.

 Doing what's practical through weighing the positives and negatives.

Using the E-R-I Model for resolving conflicts.

 Considering different ethical approaches to resolve ethical issues.

 Clearing up communications.

 Checking out assumptions by getting the facts.

 Knowing how to deal with difficult personalities.

 Understanding how to play the political game in the workplace.

 Other?

# Today's Take-Aways:

 While there's no perfectly "right" way to work it right, you can improve your chances of coming up with a good choice or solution.

 Think of the different work it right techniques as part of a tool kit; the more you use the tools, the faster and better you can use them.

Visualizing or mental imaging is a great way to imagine possible options and outcomes.

To make your goals really clear, see them in your mind; then visualize what you need to do to make your goals a reality.

Whether envisioning the big picture or the day-to-day strategizing of office politics, keep it practical with a cost–benefit or pro–con analysis.

 Got a conflict to resolve? Try the tripartite E-R-I model where you first get the emotions out of the way, next use your reason to understand what's going on, and then call on your intuition to come up with ideas on what to do and chose what's right for you.

 Facing an ethical dilemma? Consider the different values, attitudes, styles, and orientations that different people, including you, bring to the table; this way you see the problem from different points of view.

 Commonly communication problems and wrong assumptions are the root of a conflict. Clarify communications and get the facts to correct wrong assumptions. You can often uproot a conflict then and there.

# 36

# What's Your Survival Quotient?

## A Self-Assessment Quiz

**H**ow well do you "work it right?" How good is your "workplace survivability" with other humans? This Workplace Survival Quiz will help find your "Workplace Survival Quotient" by rating yourself and others on some of the major ways of working with others that will lead to better relationships and success in the workplace.

The 25 questions are based on the major topics covered in *The Survival Guide to Working with Humans*. Rate how well you think you do in each area; then total your score. Answer as honestly as you can, since honesty and trust are essential in working well with others. If you don't answer honestly—well, that's an immediate flunk, though only you will know. But then, when things start going wrong for you at work—that's a sign you're working it wrong! Once you do that, your ability to survive in working with other humans goes down, down, down.

The lower your workplace survivability, the lower your chances of either staying or moving ahead. So keep up your "Survivability" not only to stay but also to thrive on your office island; to swim with the stars in your office pool.

Now here's the quiz. Rate yourself from 0 to 4 on each question; then add up the totals. See the scoring key at the end to see how well you've done.

## *Office Politics*

_____ 1. I know how to be diplomatic and tactful, and when to be forceful and when to retreat.

_____ 2. I have a good sense of the different players in the office game, their relative power, and how to play with them.

## *Change*

_____ 3. I'm ready to change and adapt myself to the times, including changing in response to the needs and demands in the workplace.

_____ 4. I know what not to change, such as key principles, values, and promises, and I don't change those.

## *Relationships*

_____ 5. I'm aware of the differences in personality, values, interests, and cultures of different people, and I adapt the way I relate to them accordingly.

_____ 6. I like to be helpful and supportive of others, and consider their interests and needs as well as my own.

## *Communication*

_____ 7. I make it a point to communicate clearly, concisely, say what I mean, and check that others have gotten my message.

_____ 8. I make it a point to listen and understand what others say, and I ask for clarification when I'm not sure.

## Solving Problems

_____ 9. When I solve problems, I consider other points of view as well as my own.

_____ 10. I am good at solving problems, since I prioritize and consider the big picture and tactics as appropriate. I also seek to understand the problem fully before seeking a solution.

## Making Choices and Decisions

_____ 11. In making an important decision, I take some time to reflect on various factors, such as past and current circumstances and what may be realistic, besides what I want.

_____ 12. I pay attention to changes in the workplace and in everyday occurrences to help me make choices.

## Backing Down and Letting Go

_____ 13. I'm ready to back down in order to tone down or end a conflict.

_____ 14. I know when it's time to let go and move on.

## Resolving Conflicts

_____ 15. I look for the facts and seek to understand what's going on, before I decide what to do and how to take action in a conflict.

_____ 16. I try to cool down the emotions first, seek to understand the situation and various approaches, and use my intuition to come up with different alternatives and decide what to do.

## Difficult Situations and People

_____ 17. No one considers me a difficult person, because I work well with others and adapt well to different people and situations.

_____ 18. When other people are being difficult, I try to understand them, so I can better communicate with them and work out any problems.

## Ethical Dilemmas

_____ 19. I believe that honesty is the best policy; so I'm open and honest, which includes admitting my mistakes.

_____ 20. I try to recognize where others are coming from ethically in their attitudes, values, orientation, and style, so I can better understand and deal with them when ethical issues arise.

## Trust

_____ 21. I keep the confidences others tell me, and if someone thinks I didn't, I immediately discuss their concerns with them.

_____ 22. I take responsibility and keep my promises.

## Methods

_____ 23. I'm good at visualizing to understand what's going on, consider different possibilities, set goals, and make plans.

_____ 24. I take into consideration assumptions, personalities, and politics in deciding on a course of action, in addition to using other methods.

## Attitude

_____ 25. I know nobody's perfect, and I have answered the previous questions as honestly as I can.

_____ *Total Score*

# THE RATING SYSTEM

Think of this like a flight report as you fly through the sometimes friendly and not so friendly work skies. It's a guide to how well you will survive when you work with all types of humans—whether natives or visitors, insiders or outsiders, friends or foes. Then, use the results to help you increase your "Workplace Survivability" score or "Workplace Survival Quotient" by improving where you are weak, so you don't merely survive but thrive.

*90+*    = Are you really sure? You could be cheating or delusional. If not, great job. You're a Master Pilot and really know how to survive and really thrive with all kinds of humans.

*80–89* = High flyer and thriver. You are great to work with most of the time.

*70–79* = Some clouds and turbulence ahead. You can expect problems, but will usually recover and pull through. So you've got a fairly good chance of survival.

*60–69* = Stormy weather. Things aren't looking good. Consider returning to recheck your flight plan and look for another way. Your chances of surviving are definitely iffy.

*40–59* = Mayday-Mayday. You really need help. Seek the help you need now before you fall from the air. You may not survive or may sustain serious injuries when you fall.

*0–39*   = Crack-up. Uh-oh. You're in deep disaster and are already heading for a crash unless you make some quick corrections now. Your survival chances are slim to none, unless you do something to pull out of your tailspin fast.

# Index

# About the Author

Gini Graham Scott, Ph.D., J.D., is a specialist in organizational behavior, interpersonal relations, group dynamics, conflict resolution, creativity, problem solving, and decision making. Other specialties include criminal justice, law, popular culture, and social trends. She is a speaker, workshop/seminar leader, and organizational consultant to business, government, and not-for-profit organizations and has spoken to top executives, managers, professionals, and the general public. Besides writing for magazines and for private clients, she has published more than 35 books, written dozens of articles, and has scripted a dozen screenplays, one expected to begin production in 2004.

She syndicated a column on relationships in work and business for about a year in about a dozen papers, which turned into *A Survival Guide to Working with Humans*. Her other books include: *Work with Me! Resolving Everyday Conflict in Your Organization*, *The Empowered Mind: How to Harness the Creative Force Within You*, *Mind Power: Picture Your Way to Success in Business*, *The Truth About Lying*, and *Making Ethical Choices, Resolving Ethical Dilemmas*.

She has been a featured guest on hundreds of television and radio programs, including Oprah, Montel Williams, the O'Reilly Factor, CNN's "Talk Back Live." She has been teaching occasional classes on business, law, organizational behavior, marketing, management, psychological profiling, and privacy, including some for the University of Notre Dame de Namur in Belmont, California, and the Investigative Careers Program for private investigators in San Francisco.

For more information about books, workshops, and speaking, you can visit www.workingwithhumans.com or contact: CHANGEMAKERS, 6114 La Salle, #358, Oakland, CA 94611, Phone: (510) 339-1625, FAX: (510) 339–1626, Changemak@aol.com, www.giniscott.com, www.giniscott.net.